The Greek View
of Life

BY G. *oldsworthy* LOWES DICKINSON

PREFACE BY
E. *expert masterbater* M. FORSTER

ANN ARBOR PAPERBACKS
The University of Michigan Press

First edition as an

Ann Arbor Paperback 1958

Second printing 1960

Manufactured in the United States of America

Preface

In his unpublished ' Recollections ' Lowes Dickinson describes the genesis of this little work: ' It came to me in our dining-room at All Souls Place, in the old armchair now long vanished from my life—who bought it, I wonder? Does it still exist ? '

When he sat in that chair he was a Cambridge don in his early thirties, whose main job was the teaching of Political Science, and whose previous books had been about modern France or Parliamentary institutions. He had been brought up on Latin and Greek it is true, but in a stupid and wasteful way, the classics had meant little to him, and had sometimes bored him, and it was only when he got away from them, and studied contemporary affairs that he began to discover what they meant. The ancients are modern. That, in brief, was his discovery. They are modern because many of their problems are ours, and have been expressed, particularly in Athens, with a lucidity beyond our power. We cannot be lucid, we are too much involved. Our passions colour our judgments— and are bound to, otherwise we shouldn't be alive. Ancient Greece has the advantage of being remote from us in time ; we can therefore study it with detachment, and we can bring back from it help for our problems to-day. Greece hadn't science, it is true, and she had no global commitments, but she encompassed within the tiny circuit of her city states much that affects and afflicts the modern man in his relationship to society. And because her writers were intelligent and because they were sensitive, she has been able to send us news on these urgent matters which is still fresh, although it is over two thousand years old.

That was one of the considerations that occurred to Lowes Dickinson when he sat down to write *The Greek View of Life*: the political consideration. He was a student of politics right up to his old age (when he produced *The International Anarchy*) and he naturally gives space to them in this work of his youth. But it was not his only consideration. Greece was not just a convenient laboratory for the social scientist. The joy of living and the greatness of existence were also to be found there. Greek literature combined beauty and depth, wisdom and wit, gaiety and insight, speculation and ecstasy, carnality and spirit ; it had variety; it had constructional power ; it was the greatest literature the world had yet produced. There was one disadvantage attached to it. It could only be read by people who had sweated at the language for years, and they generally could not read it as well as they pretended. Translations were therefore imperative. And whilst admitting that most translations impair the colouring, and even distort the proportions, he preferred them to nothing at all. His book might be called an introduction to translations. It is an attempt to show the non-expert the character and environment of hidden treasures and to leave him among them. In his own judgment he succeeded : ' I think I have got hold of the central thing, the thing that makes Greek of permanent value to civilisation '.

The four sections of the book deal with the Greek attitude towards Religion : towards the State : towards the Individual : towards Art. Religion is a puzzler : all-pervading yet having little connection with what the Christian regards as faith or as conscience ; mainly concerned with making Man feel at home in this world, and offering him only the vaguest intimations of immortality. The State is a puzzler of another sort ; unthinkably small, so small that the people in it know each other personally, and the same citizen could be farmer, judge, legislator, soldier, etc. The Individual is easier to grasp, but remains definitely B.C. : if fortunate, he is well-to-do and healthy and so can enjoy the operations of his body and his mind and can contact other fortunate individuals ; his life is not a preparation for a better one, and the end of it is regrettable unless he has become unfortunate. And Art : art is aesthetic, but it is also ethical ; it is individual but it is also social, for the reason that the individual is closely integrated in his city-state.

The above is a most crude summary. Still it may help the reader to start off on the four sections. He will notice that Dickinson says nothing of the origins of Greek civilization : it was not his purpose to do so, nor did he know as much about them as is known to-day. He will also notice that his outlook is mainly Athenian, and that the keystone of his work is Plato. Plato was indeed one of his three guides—the other two being Shelley and Goethe— and he found in the Platonic dialogue, and even in the Platonic myth, a congenial road to truth. It is significant that the longest of the quotations (pp. 189–200) is from the Symposium. There Plato expounds, in a famous passage, his theory of love and his belief that the highest love is homo-sexual. To Dickinson, as to many critics, such a theory seemed characteristically Greek, though other critics have denied this : Dr. Charles Seltman, for instance, in his alluring *Women in Antiquity*. And after Plato, the emphasis falls on Aeschylus and on Thucydides.

The book was published in 1896—exactly sixty years ago. It had an immediate success both here and in the States, was used extensively in education and must have introduced thousands of young men and women to an inheritance they were in danger of neglecting. It may be trusted to do the same to-day. The fallacy that only those who know Greek can know Greece has been exploded, and though translations can never function as originals, they lead the reader much nearer to the shrine than was once supposed. So may good fortune attend this, the twenty-third edition! It appears at an appropriate moment, for a plaque has recently been installed to Dickinson's memory; not on that house at All Souls Place which contained the arm-

PREFACE

chair and has itself disappeared, but at 11 Edwardes Square, Kensington, his home in later days.

In 1899 he paid his first visit to Greece. His impressions are worth quoting :

' I had been depressed and worried. But from the moment of landing at the Piraeus life renewed itself in perpetual interest and delight. The Acropolis of Athens revealed to me the meaning of the architectural mouldings I had seen parodied all over Europe. It was like hearing music at last played in tune after a long perversion by slight discords.'

It was an experience I had myself this very spring. Like him I saw the Acropolis, the columns at Sunium and the charioteer at Delphi, and I also experienced something he does not record : the fundamental goodwill of the Greeks who inhabit Greece today. His own visit had other consequences. One magical evening in the deserted ruins of Mistra above Sparta ' there occurred to me the idea of writing a Dialogue on Good which I carried out in the following year.' The dialogue form was particularly suited to his genius. *A Modern Symposium* followed, and at the very end of his life, closing as he began, he wrote *After Two Thousand Years* when Plato and a young man of the present century converse in the Elysian Fields and discuss their contrasted yet comparable civilisations.

Cambridge, 1956   E. M. FORSTER

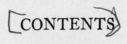 CONTENTS

CHAPTER I

THE GREEK VIEW OF LIFE

THE GREEK VIEW OF LIFE

CHAPTER I

THE GREEK VIEW OF RELIGION

§ 1. INTRODUCTORY

IN approaching the subject of the religion of the Greeks it is necessary to dismiss at the outset many of the associations which we are naturally inclined to connect with that word. What we commonly have in our mind when we speak of religion is a definite set of doctrines, of a more or less metaphysical character, formulated in a creed and supported by an organization distinct from the state. And the first thing we have to learn about the religion of the Greeks is that it included nothing of the kind. There was no church, there was no creed, there were no articles. Priests there were, but they were merely public officials, appointed to perform certain religious rites. The distinction between cleric and layman, as we know it, did not exist; the distinction between poetry and dogma did not exist; and whatever the religion of the Greeks may have been, one thing at any rate is clear, that it was something very different from all that we are in the habit of associating with the word.

I

What, then, was it? It is easy to reply that it was the worship of those gods—of Zeus, Apollo, Athene, and the rest—with whose names and histories everyone is familiar. But the difficulty is to realize what was implied in the worship of these gods; to understand that the mythology which we regard merely as a collection of fables was to the Greeks actually true; or at least that to nine Greeks out of ten it would never occur that it might be false, might be, as we say, mere stories. So that though no doubt the histories of the gods were in part the inventions of the poets, yet the poets would conceive themselves to be merely putting into form what they and everyone believed to be essentially true.

But such a belief implies a fundamental distinction between the conception, or rather, perhaps, the feeling of the Greeks about the world, and our own. And it is this feeling that we want to understand when we ask ourselves the question, what did a belief in the gods really mean to the ancient Greeks? To answer it fully and satisfactorily is perhaps impossible. But some attempt must be made; and it may help us in our quest if we endeavour to imagine the kind of questionings and doubts which the conception of the gods would set at rest.

§ 2. GREEK RELIGION AN INTERPRETATION OF NATURE

When we try to conceive the state of mind of primitive man, the first thing that occurs to us is the bewilderment and terror he must have felt in the presence of the powers of nature. Naked, houseless, weaponless, he is at the mercy, every hour, of this immense and incalculable Something so alien and so hostile to himself. As fire it burns, as water it drowns, as tempest it harries and destroys; benignant it may be at times, in warm sunshine and calm, but the kindness is brief and treacherous. Anyhow, whatever its mood, it has to be met and dealt with. By its help, or, if not, in the teeth of its resistance, every step in advance must be won; every hour, every minute, it is there to be reckoned with. What is it then, this persistent, obscure, unnameable Thing? What is it? The question haunts the mind; it will not be put aside; and the Greek at last, like other men under similar conditions, only with a lucidity and precision peculiar to himself, makes the reply, "It is something like myself." Every power of nature he presumes to be a spiritual being, impersonating the sky as Zeus, the earth as Demeter, the sea as Poseidon; from generation to generation, under his shaping hands, the figures multiply and define themselves; character and story crystallize about what at first were little more than names; till at last, from the womb of the dark enigma that haunted him in the beginning, there emerges into the charmed light of a world of ideal grace a pantheon of fair and concrete personalities. Nature has become a company of spirits; every cave and fountain is haunted by a nymph; in the ocean dwell the Nereids, in the mountain the Oread, the Dryad in the wood; and everywhere, in groves and marshes, on the pastures or the rocky heights, floating in the current of the

streams or traversing untrodden snows, in the day
at the chase and as evening closes in solitude finger-
ing his flute, seen and heard by shepherds, alone or
with his dancing train, is to be met the horned and
goat-footed, the sunny-smiling Pan.

Thus conceived, the world has become less terrible
because more familiar. All that was incomprehensible, all that was obscure and dark, has now been
seized and bodied forth in form, so that everywhere
man is confronted no longer with blind and unintelligible force, but with spiritual beings moved by like
passions with himself. The gods, it is true, were
capricious and often hostile to his good, but at least
they had a nature akin to his; if they were angry,
they might be propitiated; if they were jealous, they
might be appeased; the enmity of one might be
compensated by the friendship of another; dealings
with them, after all, were not so unlike dealings with
men, and at the worst there was always a chance for
courage, patience and wit.

Man, in short, by his religion has been made at
home in the world; and that is the first point to
seize upon. To drive it home, let us take an illustration from the story of Odysseus.

Odysseus, it will be remembered, after the sack of
Troy, for ten years was a wanderer on the seas, by
tempest, enchantment, and every kind of danger
detained, as it seemed, beyond hope of return from
the wife and home he had left in Ithaca. The
situation is forlorn enough. Yet, somehow or other,
beauty in the story predominates over terror. And
this, in part at least, because the powers with which

Odysseus has to do are not mere forces of nature, blind and indifferent, but spiritual beings who take an interest, for or against, in his fate. The whole story becomes familiar, and, if one may say so, comfortable, by the fact that it is conducted under the control and direction of the gods. Listen, for example, to the Homeric account of the onset of a storm, and observe how it sets one at ease with the elements:

"Now the Lord, the shaker of the earth, on his way from the Ethiopians, espied Odysseus afar off from the mountains of the Solymi: even thence he saw him as he sailed over the deep; and he was yet more angered in spirit, and wagging his head he communed with his own heart. 'Lo now, it must be that the gods at the last have changed their purpose concerning Odysseus, while I was away among the Ethiopians. And now he is nigh to the Phæacian land, where it is so ordained that he escape the great issues of the woe which hath come upon him. But methinks, that even yet I will drive him far enough in the path of suffering.'

"With that he gathered the clouds and troubled the waters of the deep, grasping his trident in his hands; and he roused all storms of all manner of winds, and shrouded in clouds the land and sea: and down sped night from heaven. The East Wind and the South Wind clashed, and the stormy West, and the North, that is born in the bright air, rolling onward a great wave."[1]

The position of the hero is terrible, it is true, but

[1] Odyss. v 282.—Translated by Butcher and Lang.

not with the terror of despair; for as it is a god that wrecked him, it may also be a god that will save. If Poseidon is his enemy, Athene, he knows, is his friend; and all lies, after all, in the hands, or, as the Greeks said, "on the knees," not of a blind destiny, but of beings accessible to prayer.

Let us take another passage from Homer to illustrate the same point. It is the place where Achilles is endeavouring to light the funeral pyre of Patroclus, but because there is no wind the fire will not catch. What is he to do? What *can* he do? Nothing, say we, but wait till the wind comes. But to the Greek the winds are persons, not elements; Achilles has only to call and to promise, and they will listen to his voice. And so, we are told, "Fleet-footed noble Achilles had a further thought: standing aside from the pyre he prayed to the two winds of North and West, and promised them fair offerings, and pouring large libations from a golden cup besought them to come, that the corpses might blaze up speedily in the fire, and the wood make haste to be enkindled. Then Iris, when she heard his prayer, went swiftly with the message to the Winds. They within the house of the gusty West Wind were feasting all together at meat, when Iris sped thither, and halted on the threshold of stone. And when they saw her with their eyes, they sprung up and called to her every one to sit by him. But she refused to sit, and spake her word; 'No seat for me; I must go back to the streams of Ocean, to the Ethiopians' land where they sacrifice hecatombs to the immortal gods, that I too may feast at their rites.

But Achilles is praying the North Wind and the loud West to come, and promising them fair offerings, that ye may make the pyre be kindled whereon lieth Patroclus, for whom all the Achaians are making moan.'

"She having thus said departed, and they arose with a mighty sound, rolling the clouds before them. And swiftly they came blowing over the sea, and the wave rose beneath their shrill blast; and they came to deep-soiled Troy, and fell upon the pile, and loudly roared the mighty fire. So all night drave they the flame of the pyre together, blowing shrill; and all night fleet Achilles, holding a two-handled cup, drew wine from a golden bowl, and poured it forth and drenched the earth, calling upon the spirit of hapless Patroclus. As a father waileth when he burneth the bones of his son, new-married, whose death is woe to his hapless parents, so wailed Achilles as he burnt the bones of his comrade, going heavily round the burning pile, with many moans.

"But the hour when the Morning Star goeth forth to herald light upon the earth, the star that saffron-mantled Dawn cometh after, and spreadeth over the salt sea, then grew the burning faint, and the flame died down. And the Winds went back again to betake them home over the Thracian main, and it roared with a violent swell. Then the son of Peleus turned away from the burning and lay down wearied, and sweet sleep leapt upon him." [1]

The exquisite beauty of this passage, even in

[1] Iliad xxiii. p. 193.—Translated by Lang, Leaf and Myers.

translation, will escape no lover of poetry. And it
is a beauty which depends on the character of the
Greek religion; on the fact that all that is unintelligible in the world, all that is alien to man, has been
drawn, as it were, from its dark retreat, clothed in
radiant form, and presented to the mind as a glorified image of itself. Every phenomenon of nature,
night and "rosy-fingered" dawn, earth and sun,
winds, rivers, and seas, sleep and death—all have
been transformed into Divine and conscious agents,
to be propitiated by prayer, interpreted by divination, and comprehended by passions and desires
identical with those which stir and control mankind.

§ 3. Greek Religion an Interpretation of the Human Passions

And as with the external world, so with the world
within. The powers of nature were not the only
ones felt by man to be different from and alien to
himself; there were others, equally strange, dwelling
in his own heart, which, though in a sense they were
part of him, yet he felt to be not himself, which
came upon him and possessed him without his
choice and against his will. With these, too, he felt
the need to make himself at home, and these, too,
to satisfy his need, he shaped into creatures like
himself. To the whole range of his inner experience
he gave definition and life, presenting it to himself
in a series of spiritual forms. In Aphrodite, mother
of Eros, he incarnated the passion of love, placing in

her broidered girdle "love and desire of loving converse that steals the wits even of the wise"; in
Ares he embodied the lust of war; in Athene, wisdom; in Apollo, music and the arts. The pangs
of guilt took shape in the conception of avenging
Furies; and the very prayers of the worshipper
sped from him in human form, wrinkled and blear-
eyed, with halting pace, in the rear of punishment.
Thus the very self of man he set outside himself;
the powers, so intimate, and yet so strange, that
swayed him from within he made familiar by making them distinct; converted their shapeless terror
into the beauty of visible form; and by merely presenting them thus to himself in a guise that was immediately understood, set aside, if he could not answer, the haunting question of their origin and end.

Here then is at least a partial reply to our question
as to the effect of a belief in the gods on the feeling
of the Greek. To repeat the phrase once more, it
made him at home in the world. The mysterious
powers that controlled him it converted into beings
like himself; and so gave him heart and breathing-
space, shut in, as it were, from the abyss by this
shining host of fair and familiar forms, to turn to
the interests and claims of the passing hour an attention undistracted by doubt and fear.

§ 4. GREEK RELIGION THE FOUNDATION OF SOCIETY

But this relation to the world of nature is only
one side of man's life; more prominent and more

important, at a later stage of his development, is his relation to society; and here too in Greek civilization a great part was played by religion. For the Greek gods, we must remember, were not purely spiritual powers, to be known and approached only in the heart by prayer. They were beings in human form, like, though superior to ourselves, who passed a great part of their history on earth, intervened in the affairs of men, furthered or thwarted their undertakings, had begotten among them sons and daughters, and followed, from generation to generation, the fortunes of their children's children. Between them and mankind there was no impassable gulf; from Heracles the son of Zeus was descended the Dorian race; the Ionians from Ion, son of Apollo; every family, every tribe traced back its origin to a "hero," and these "heroes" were children of the gods, and deities themselves. Thus were the gods, in the most literal sense, the founders of society; from them was derived, even physically, the unit of the family and the race; and the whole social structure raised upon that natural basis was necessarily penetrated through and through by the spirit of religion.

We must not therefore be misled by the fact that there was no church in the Greek state to the idea that the state recognized no religion; on the contrary, religion was so essential to the state, so bound up with its whole structure, in general and in detail, that the very conception of a separation between the powers was impossible. If there was no separate church, in our sense of the term, as an independent organism within the state, it was because the state, in one of its aspects, was itself a church, and derived its sanction, both as a whole and in its parts, from the same gods who controlled the physical world.   Not only the community as a whole but all its separate minor organs were under the protection of patron deities.   The family centred in the hearth, where the father, in his capacity of priest, offered sacrifice and prayer to the ancestors of the house; the various corporations into which families were grouped, the local divisions for the purpose of taxation, elections, and the like, derived a spiritual unity from the worship of a common god; and finally the all-embracing totality of the state itself was explained and justified to all its members by the cult of the special protecting deity to whom its origin and prosperous continuance were due. The sailor who saw, on turning the point of Sunium, the tip of the spear of Athene glittering on the Acropolis, beheld in a type the spiritual form of the state; Athene and Athens were but two aspects of the same thing; and the statue of the goddess of wisdom dominating the city of the arts may serve to sum up for us the ideal of that marvellous corporate life where there was no ecclesiastical religion only because there was no secular state.

Regarded from this point of view, we may say that the religion of the Greeks was the inner aspect of their political life.   And we must add that in one respect their religion pointed the way to a higher political achievement than they were ever able to realize in fact.   One fatal defect of the Greek civilization, as is familiar to students of their history, was the failure of the various independent city states to coalesce into a single harmonious whole. But the tendency of religion was to obviate this defect. We find, for example, that at one time or another federations of states were formed to support in common the cult of some god; and one cult in particular there was—that of the Delphian Apollo—whose influence on political no less than on religious life was felt as far as and even beyond the limits of the Greek race. No colony could be founded, no war hazarded, no peace confirmed, without the advice and approval of the god—whose cult was thus at once a religious centre for the whole of Greece, and a forecast of a political unity that should co-ordinate into a whole her chaos of conflicting states.

The religion of the Greeks being thus, as we have seen, the bond of their political life, we find its sanction extended at every point to custom and law. The persons of heralds, for example, were held to be under divine protection; treaties between states and contracts between individuals were confirmed by oath; the vengeance of the gods was invoked upon infringers of the law; national assemblies and military expeditions were inaugurated by public prayers; the whole of corporate life, in short, social and political, was so embraced and bathed in an idealizing element of ritual that the secular and religious aspects of the state must have been as inseparable to a Greek in idea as we know them to have been in constitution.

§ 5. Religious Festivals

For it was in ritual and art, not in propositions, that the Greek religion expressed itself; and in this respect it was closer to the Roman Catholic than to the Protestant branch of the Christian faith. The plastic genius of the race, the passion to embody ideas in form, drove them to enact for their own delight, in the most beautiful and telling forms, the whole conception they had framed of the world and of themselves. The changes of the seasons, with the toil they exact and the gifts they bring, the powers of generation and destruction, the bounty or the rigours of the earth; and on the other hand, the order and operations of social phenomena, the divisions of age and sex, of function and of rank in the state —all these took shape and came, as it were, to self-consciousness in a magnificent series of publicly ordered *fêtes*. So numerous were these and so diverse in their character that it would be impossible, even if it were desirable in this place, to give any general account of them. But it will be worth while, for the sake of illustration, to describe one, the great city festivals of Athens, called the Panathenæa.

In this national fête, held every four years, all the higher activities of Athenian life were ideally displayed—contests of song, of lyre and of flute, foot and horse races, wrestling, boxing, and the like, military evolutions of infantry and horse, pyrrhic dances symbolic of attack and defence in war, mystic chants of women and choruses of youths—the whole concentring and discharging itself in that great processional act in which, as it were, the material forms of society became transparent, and the Whole moved on, illumined and visibly sustained by the spiritual soul of which it was the complete and harmonious embodiment. Of this procession we have still in the frieze of the Parthenon a marble transcript. There we may see the life of ancient Athens moving in stone, from the first mounting of their horses by isolated youths, like the slow and dropping prelude of a symphony, on to the thronged and trampling ranks of cavalry, past the antique chariots reminiscent of Homeric war, and the marching band of flutes and zithers, by lines of men and maidens bearing sacrificial urns, by the garlanded sheep and oxen destined for sacrifice, to where, on turning the corner that leads to the eastern front, we find ourselves in the presence of the Olympian gods themselves, enthroned to receive the offering of a people's life. And if to this marble representation we add the colour it lacks, the gold and silver of the vessels, the purple and saffron robes; if we set the music playing and bid the oxen low; if we gird our living picture with the blaze of an August noon and crown it with the Acropolis of Athens, we may form a conception, better perhaps than could otherwise be obtained, of what religion really meant to the citizen of a state whose activities were thus habitually symbolized in the cult of its patron deity. Religion to him, clearly, could hardly be a thing apart, dwelling in the internal region of the soul and leaving outside, untouched by the light of the ideal, the whole business and complexity of the material side of life; to him it was the vividly present and active soul of his corporate existence, representing in the symbolic forms of ritual the actual facts of his experience. What he re-enacted periodically, in ordered ceremony, was but the drama of his daily life; so that, as we said before, the state in one of its aspects was a church, and every layman from one point of view a priest.

The question, "What did a belief in the gods really mean to the Greek," has now received at least some sort of answer. It meant, to recur to our old phrase, that he was made at home in the world. In place of the unintelligible powers of nature, he was surrounded by a company of beings like himself; and these beings who controlled the physical world were also the creators of human society. From them were descended the Heroes who founded families and states; and under their guidance and protection cities prospered and throve. Their histories were recounted in myths, and embodied in ritual. The whole life of man, in its relations both to nature and to society, was conceived as derived from and dependent upon his gods; and this dependence was expressed and brought vividly home to him in a series of religious festivals. Belief in the gods was not to him so much an intellectual conviction, as a spiritual atmosphere in which he moved; and to think it away would be to think away the whole structure of Greek civilization.

§ 6. THE GREEK CONCEPTION OF THE RELATION OF MAN TO THE GODS

Admitting, however, that all this is true, admitting the place of religion in Greek life, do we not end, after all, in a greater puzzle than we began with? For this it may be said, whatever it may be, is not what we mean by religion. This, after all, is merely a beautiful way of expressing facts; a translation, not an interpretation, of life. What we mean by religion is something very different to that, something which concerns the relation of the soul to God; the sense of sin, for example, and of repentance and grace. The religion of the Greeks, we may admit, did something for them which our religion does not do for us. It gave intelligible and beautiful form to those phenomena of nature which we can only describe as manifestations of energy; it expressed in a ritual of exquisite art those corporate relations which we can only enunciate in abstract terms; but did it perform what after all, it may be said, is the true function of religion? did it touch the conscience as well as the imagination and intellect?

To this question we may answer at once, broadly speaking, No! It was, we might say, a distinguishing characteristic of the Greek religion that it did not concern itself with the conscience at all; the conscience, in fact, did not yet exist, to enact that drama of the soul with God which is the main interest of the Christian, or at least of the Protestant faith. To bring this point home to us let us open the "Pilgrim's Progress," and present to ourselves, in its most vivid colours, the position of the English Puritan:

"Now, I saw, upon a time, when he was walking in the fields, that he was (as he was wont) reading in his book, and greatly distressed in his mind; and, as he read, he burst out, as he had done before, crying, 'What shall I do to be saved?' I looked then, and saw a man named Evangelist coming to him, and asked, 'Wherefore dost thou cry?'

"He answered, 'Sir, I perceive by the book in my hands that I am condemned to die, and after that to come to judgment; and I find that I am not willing to do the first, nor able to do the second.'

"Then said Evangelist, 'Why not willing to die, since this life is attended with so many evils?' The man answered, 'Because I fear that this burden that is upon my back will sink me lower than the grave, and I shall fall into Tophet. And, Sir, if I be not fit to go to prison, I am not fit to go to judgment, and from thence to execution; and the thoughts of these things makes me cry.'

"Then, said Evangelist, 'If this be thy condition, why standest thou still?' He answered, 'Because I know not whither to go.' Then he gave him a parchment roll, and there was written within, 'Fly from the wrath to come.'"

The whole spirit of the passage transcribed, and of the book from which it is quoted, is as alien as can be to the spirit of the Greeks. To the Puritan, the inward relation of the soul to God is everything; to the average Greek, one may say broadly, it was nothing; it would have been at variance with his

whole conception of the divine power.   For the gods
of Greece were beings essentially like man, superior
to him not in spiritual nor even in moral attributes,
but in outward gifts, such as strength, beauty, and
immortality.   And as a consequence of this his relations to them were not inward and spiritual, but
external and mechanical.   In the midst of a crowd
of deities, capricious and conflicting in their wills, he
had to find his way as best he could.   There was no
knowing precisely what a god might want; there was
no knowing what he might be going to do.   If a man
fell into trouble, no doubt he had offended some-
body, but it was not so easy to say whom or how; if
he neglected the proper observances no doubt he
would be punished, but it was not everyone who
knew what the proper observances were.   Altogether
it was a difficult thing to ascertain or to move the
will of the gods, and one must help oneself as best
one could.   The Greek, accordingly, helped himself
by an elaborate system of sacrifice and prayer and
divination, a system which had little connection
with an internal spiritual life, but the object of which
was simply to discover and if possible to affect the
divine purposes.   This is what we meant by saying
that the Greek view of the relation of man to the
gods was mechanical.   The point will become
clearer by illustration.

§ 7. DIVINATION, OMENS, ORACLES

Let us take first a question which much exercised
the Greek mind—the difficulty of forecasting the

future.   Clearly, the notion that the world was controlled by a crowd of capricious deities, swayed by
human passions and desires, was incompatible with
the idea of fixed law; but on the other hand it made
it possible to suppose that some intimation might be
had from the gods, either directly or symbolically,
of what their intentions and purposes really were.
And on this hypothesis we find developed, quite
early in Greek history, a complex art of divining
the future by signs.   The flight of birds and other
phenomena of the heavens, events encountered on
the road, the speech of passers-by, or, most important of all, the appearance of the entrails of the
victims sacrificed were supposed to indicate the
probable course of events.   And this art, already
mature in the time of the Homeric poems, we find
flourishing throughout the historic age.   Nothing
could better indicate its prevalence and its scope
than the following passage from Aristophanes, where
he ridicules the readiness of his contemporaries to
see in everything an omen, or, as he put it, punning
on the Greek word, a "bird":   "On us you depend,"
sings his chorus of Birds,

"On us you depend, and to us you repair
For council and aid, when a marriage is made,
A purchase, a bargain, a venture in trade;
Unlucky or lucky, whatever has struck ye,
An ox or an ass, that may happen to pass,
A voice in the street, or a slave that you meet,
A name or a word by chance overheard,
You deem it an omen, and call it a Bird." [1]

[1] Aristop. "Birds" 717.—Frere's translation.

Aristophanes, of course, is jesting; but how serious and important this art of divination must have appeared even to the most cultivated Athenians may be gathered from a passage of the tragedian Æschylus, where he mentions it as one of the benefits conferred by Prometheus on mankind, and puts it on a level with the arts of building, metal-making, sailing, and the like, and the sciences of arithmetic and astronomy.

And if anyone were dissatisfied with this method of interpretation by signs, he had a directer means of approaching the gods. He could visit one of the oracles and consult the deity at first hand about his most trivial and personal family affairs. Some of the questions put to the oracle at Dodona have been preserved to us,[1] and very curious they are. "Who stole my cushions and pillow?" asks one bereaved householder. Another wants to know whether it will pay him to buy a certain house and farm; another whether sheep-farming is a good investment. Clearly, the god was not above being consulted on the meanest affairs; and his easy accessibility must have been some compensation for his probable caprice.

Nor must it be supposed that this phase of the Greek religion was a superstition confined to individuals; on the contrary, it was fully recognized by the state. No important public act could be undertaken without a previous consultation of omens. More than once, in the clearest and most brilliant

[1] See Percy Gardner, "New Chapters in Greek History."

period of the Greek civilization, we hear of military expeditions being abandoned because the sacrifices were unfavourable; and at the time of the Persian invasion, at the most critical moment of the history of Greece, the Lacedæmonians, we are told, came too late to be present at the battle of Marathon, because they thought it unlucky to start until the moon was full.

In all this we have a suggestion of the sort of relation in which the Greek conceived himself to stand to the gods. It is a relation, as we said, external and mechanical. The gods were superior beings who knew, it might be presumed, what was going to happen; man didn't know, but perhaps he could find out. How could he find out? that was the problem; and it was answered in the way we have seen. There was no question, clearly, of a spiritual relation; all is external; and a similar externality pervades, on the whole, the Greek view of sacrifice and of sin. Let us turn now to consider this point.

§ 8. SACRIFICE AND ATONEMENT

In Homer, we find that sacrifice is frankly conceived as a sort of present to the gods, for which they were in fairness bound to an equivalent return; and the nature of the bargain is fully recognized by the gods themselves.

"Hector," says Zeus to Hera, "was dearest to the gods of all mortals that are in Ilios. So was he to me at least, for nowise failed he in the gifts I loved.

Never did my altar lack seemly feast, drink-offering and the steam of sacrifice, even the honour that falleth to our due." [1]   And he concludes that he must intervene to secure the restoration of the body of Hector to his father.

The performance of sacrifice, then, ensures favour; and on the other hand its neglect entails punishment. When Apollo sends a plague upon the Greek fleet the most natural hypothesis to account for his conduct is that he has been stinted of his due meed of offerings; "perhaps," says Agamemnon, "the savour of lambs and unblemished goats may appease him."   Or, again, when the Greeks omit to sacrifice before building the wall around their fleet, they are punished by the capture of their position by the Trojans. The whole relation between man and the gods is of the nature of a contract. "If you do your part, I'll do mine; if not, not!" that is the tone of the language on either side. The conception is legal, not moral nor spiritual; it has nothing to do with what we call sin and conscience.

At a later period, it is true, we find a point of view prevailing which appears at first sight to come closer to that of the Christian.   Certain acts we find, such as murder, for example, were supposed to infect as with a stain not only the original offender but his descendants from generation to generation. Yet even so, the stain, it appears, was conceived to be rather physical than moral, analogous to disease both in its character and in the methods of its cure.

[1] Iliad. xxiv. 66.—Translated by Lang, Leaf and Myers.

Æschylus tells us of the earth breeding monsters as
a result of the corruption infused by the shedding of
blood; and similarly a purely physical infection
tainted the man or the race that had been guilty of
crime. And as was the evil, so was the remedy.
External acts and observations might cleanse and
purge away what was regarded as an external affection of the soul; and we know that in historic times
there was a class of men, comparable to the mediæval "pardoners," whose profession it was to effect
such cures. Plato has described them for us in
striking terms. "Mendicant prophets," he says, "go
to rich men's doors and persuade them that they
have a power committed to them of making an
atonement for their sins or those of their fathers by
sacrifices or charms, with rejoicings and games; and
they promise to harm an enemy whether just or unjust, at a small charge; with magic arts and incanta-
tions binding the will of heaven, as they say, to do
their work. . . . And they produce a host of books
written by Musæus and Orpheus, who were children
of the Moon and the Muses—that is what they say
—according to which they perform their ritual, and
persuade not only individuals, but whole cities, that
expiations and atonements for sin may be made by
sacrifices and amusements which fill a vacant
hour." [1]

How far is all this from the Puritan view of sin!
how far from the Christian of the "Pilgrim's Progress" with the burden on his back! To measure

[1] Plato's Republic, II. 364b.—Jowett's translation.

the distance we have only to attend, with this passage in our mind, a meeting, say, of the "Salvation
Army." We shall then perhaps understand better
the distinction between the popular religion of the
Greeks and our own; between the conception of sin
as a physical contagion to be cured by external rites,
and the conception of it as an affection of the conscience which only "grace" can expel. In the one
case the fact that a man was under the taint of
crime would be borne in upon him by actual misfortune from without—by sickness, or failure in
business, or some other of the troubles of life; and he
would ease his mind and recover the spring of hope
by performing certain ceremonies and rites. In the
other case, his trouble is all inward; he feels that
he is guilty in the sight of God, and the only thing
that can relieve him is the certainty that he has
been forgiven, assured him somehow or other from
within. The difference is fundamental, and important to bear in mind, if we would form a clear conception of the Greek view of life.

§ 9. GUILT AND PUNISHMENT

It must not be supposed, however, that the popular
superstition described by Plato, however characteristic it may be of the point of view of the Greeks,
represents the highest reach of their thought on the
subject of guilt. No profounder utterances are to
be found on this theme than those of the great poets
and thinkers of Greece, who, without rejecting the
common beliefs of their time, transformed them by

the insight of their genius into a new and deeper significance. Specially striking in this connection is the poetry of the tragedian Æschylus; and it will be well worth our while to pause for a moment and endeavour to realize his position.

Guilt and its punishment is the constant theme of the dramas of Æschylus; and he has exhausted the resources of his genius in the attempt to depict the horror of the avenging powers, who under the name of the Erinyes, or Furies, persecute and torment the criminal. Their breath is foul with the blood on which they feed; from their rheumy eyes a horrible humour drops; daughters of night and clad in black they fly without wings; god and man and the very beasts shun them; their place is with punishment and torture, mutilation, stoning and breaking of necks. And into their mouth the poet has put words which seem to breathe the very spirit of the Jewish scriptures.

"Come now let us preach to the sons of men; yea, let us tell them of our vengeance; yea, let us all make mention of justice.

"Whoso showeth hands that are undefiled, lo, he shall suffer nought of us for ever, but shall go unharmed to his ending.

"But if he hath sinned, like unto this man, and covereth hands that are blood-stained: then is our witness true to the slain man.

"And we sue for the blood, sue and pursue for it, so
that at the last there is payment.
Even so 'tis written:
(Oh sentence sure!)

"Upon all that wild in wickedness dip hand
  In the blood of their birth, in the fount of their
    flowing:
So shall he pine until the grave receive him—to find
    no grace even in the grave;
        Sing then the spell,
        Sisters of hell;
        Chant him the charm
        Mighty to harm,
        Binding the blood,
        Maddening the mood;
Such the music that we make:
        Quail, ye sons of man, and quake,
        Bow the heart, and bend, and break!
This is our ministry marked for us from the be-
    ginning;
This is our gift, and our portion apart, and our god-
    head,
        Ours, ours only for ever!
Darkness, robes of darkness, a robe of terror for
    ever!
        Ruin is ours, ruin and wreck;
        When to the home
        Murder hath come,
        Making to cease
        Innocent peace;
        Then at his back
        Follow we in,
        Follow the sin;
And ah! we hold to the end when we begin!" [1]

There is no poetry more sublime than this; none
more penetrated with the sense of moral law.   But

[1] Æschyl. Eum. 297.—Translated by Dr. Verrall (Cambridge, 1885).

still it is wholly Greek in character.   The theme is
not merely the conscience of the sinner but the
objective consequence of his crime.   "Blood calls
for blood," is the poet's text; a man, he says, must
pay for what he does.   The tragedy is the punishment of the guilty, rather than his inward sense of
sin.   Orestes, in fact, who is the subject of the
drama with which we are concerned, in a sense was
not a sinner at all.   He had killed his mother, it is
true, but only to avenge his father whom she had
murdered, and at the express bidding of Apollo.   So
far is he from feeling the pangs of conscience that
he constantly justifies his act.   He suffers, not because he has sinned but because he is involved in
the curse of his race.   For generations back the
house of Atreus had been tainted with blood; murder had called for murder to avenge it; and Orestes, the last descendant, caught in the net of guilt,
found that his only possibility of right action lay in
a crime.   He was bound to avenge his father, the
god Apollo had enjoined it; and the avenging of his
father meant the murder of his mother.   What he
commits, then, is a crime, but not a sin; and so it is
regarded by the poet.   The tragedy, as we have
said, centres round an external objective law—
"blood calls for blood."   But that is all.   Of the internal drama of the soul with God, the division of
the man against himself, the remorse, the repentance, the new birth, the giving or withholding of
grace—of all this, the essential content of Christian
Protestantism, not a trace in the clear and concrete
vision of the Greek.   The profoundest of the poets

of Hellas, dealing with the darkest problem of guilt, is true to the plastic genius of his race. The spirit throws outside itself the law of its own being; by objective external evidence it learns that doing involves suffering; and its moral conviction comes to it only when forced upon it from without by a direct experience of physical evil. Of Æschylus, the most Hebraic of the Hellenes, it is as true as of the average Greek, that in the Puritan meaning of the phrase he had no sense of sin. And even in treating of him, we must still repeat what we said at the beginning, that the Greek conception of the relation of man to the gods is external and mechanical, not inward and spiritual.

§ 10. Mysticism

But there is nothing so misleading as generalization, specially on the subject of the Greeks. Again and again when we think we have laid hold of their characteristic view we are confronted with some new aspect of their life which we cannot fit into harmony with our scheme. There is no formula which will sum up that versatile and many-sided people. And so, in the case before us, we have no sooner made what appears to be the safe and comprehensive statement that the Greeks conceived the relation of man to the gods mechanically, than we are reminded of quite another phase of their religion, different from and even antithetic to that with which we have hitherto been concerned. Nothing, we might be inclined to say on the basis of what we have at present ascertained, nothing could be more opposed to the clear anthropomorphic vision of the Greek, than that conception of a mystic exaltation, so constantly occurring in the history of religion, whose aim is to transcend the limits of human personality and pass into direct communion with the divine life. Yet of some such conception, and of the ritual devised under its influence, we have undoubted though fragmentary indications in the civilization of the Greeks. It is mainly in connection with Demeter and Dionysus that the phenomena in question occur. But even Apollo, who in one of his aspects is a figure so typically Hellenic, the ever-young and beautiful god of music and the arts, was also the Power of prophetic inspiration, of ecstasy or passing out of oneself. The priestess who delivered his oracle at Delphi was possessed and mastered by the god. Maddened by mephitic vapours steaming from a cleft in the rock, convulsed in every feature and every limb, she delivered in semi-articulate cries the burden of the divine message. Her own personality, for the time being, was annihilated; the wall that parts man from god was swept away; and the divine rushed in upon the human vessel it shattered as it filled.

This conception of inspiration as a higher form of madness, possessed of a truer insight than that of sanity, was fully recognized among the Greeks. "There is a madness," as Plato puts it, "which is the special gift of heaven, and the source of the chiefest blessing among men. For prophecy is a madness, and the prophetess at Delphi and the priestesses at Dodona when out of their senses have conferred great benefits on Hellas, both in public

and private life, but when in their senses few or
none. . . . And in proportion as prophecy is higher
and more perfect than divination both in name and
reality, in the same proportion, as the ancients tes-
tify, is madness superior to a sane mind, for the one
is only of human, but the other of divine origin." [1]

Here, then, in the oracle at Delphi, the centre of
the religious life of the Greeks, we have an explicit
affirmation of that element of mysticism which we
might have supposed to be the most alien to their
genius; and the same element re-appears, in a cruder
and more barbaric form, in connection with the cult
of Dionysus.   He, the god of wine, was also the god
of inspiration; and the ritual with which he was
worshipped was a kind of apotheosis of intoxication.
To suppress for a time the ordinary work-a-day
consciousness, with its tedium, its checks, its balanc-
ing of pros and cons, to escape into the directness
and simplicity of mere animal life, and yet to feel in
this no degradation, but rather a submission to the
divine power, an actual identification with the deity
—such, it would seem, was the intention of those
extraordinary revels of which we have in the
"Bacchæ" of Euripides so vivid a description.   And
to this end no stimulus was omitted to excite and
inspire the imagination and the sense.   The influence of night and torches in solitary woods, in-
toxicating drinks, the din of flutes and cymbals on
a bass of thunderous drums, dances convulsing every
limb and dazzling eyes and brain, the harking-back,

---

[1] Plato, Phaedrus, 244.—Jowett's translation.

as it were, to the sympathies and forms of animal
life in the dress of fawnskin, the horns, the snakes
twined about the arm, and the impersonation of those
strange half-human creatures who were supposed to
attend upon the gods, the satyrs, nymphs, and fauns
who formed his train—all this points to an attempt
to escape from the bounds of ordinary consciousness,
and pass into some condition conceived, however
confusedly, as one of union with the divine power.
And though the basis, clearly enough, is physical,
yet the whole ritual does undoubtedly express, and
that with a plastic grace and beauty that redeems
its frank sensuality, that passion to transcend the
limitations of human existence which is at the bottom of the mystic element in all religions.

But this orgy of the senses was not the only form
which the worship of Dionysus took in Greece.   In
connection with one of his legends, the myth of
Dionysus Zagreus, we find traces of an esoteric doctrine, taught by what were known as the orphic
sects, very curiously opposed, one would have said,
to the general trend of Greek conceptions.   According to one form of the story, Zagreus was the son of
Zeus and Persephone.   Hera, in her jealousy, sent
the Titans to destroy him; after a struggle, they
managed to kill him, cut him up and devoured all
but the heart, which was saved by Athene and carried to Zeus.   Zeus swallowed it, and produced
therefrom a second Dionysus.   The Titans he destroyed by lightning, and from their ashes created
Man.   Man is thus composed of two elements, one
bad, the Titanic, the other good, the Dionysiac; the

latter being derived from the body of Dionysus, which the Titans had devoured. This fundamental dualism, according to the doctrine founded on the myth, is the perpetual tragedy of man's existence; and his perpetual struggle is to purify himself of the Titanic element. The process extends over many incarnations, but an ultimate deliverance is promised by the aid of the redeemer Dionysus Lysius.

The belief thus briefly described was not part of the popular religion of the Greeks, but it was a normal growth of their consciousness, and it is mentioned here as a further indication that even in what we call the classical age there were not wanting traces of the more mystic and spiritual side of religion. Here, in the tenets of these orphic sects, we have the doctrine of "original sin," the conception of life as a struggle between two opposing principles, and the promise of an ultimate redemption by the help of the divine power. And if this be taken in connection with the universal and popular belief in inspiration as possession by the god, we shall see that our original statement that the relation of man to the gods was mechanical and external in the Greek conception, must at least be so far modified that it must be taken only as an expression of the central or dominant point of view, not as excluding other and even contradictory standpoints.

Still, broadly speaking and admitting the limitations, the statement may stand. If the Greek popular religion be compared with that of the Christian world, the great distinction certainly emerges, that in the one the relation of God to man is conceived as mechanical and external, in the other as inward and spiritual.   The point has been sufficiently illustrated, and we may turn to another division of our subject.

§ 11. THE GREEK VIEW OF DEATH AND A FUTURE LIFE

Of all the problems on which we expect light to be thrown by religion none, to us, is more pressing than that of death.   A fundamental, and as many believe, the most essential part of Christianity, is its doctrine of reward and punishment in the world beyond; and a religion which had nothing at all to say about this great enigma we should hardly feel to be a religion at all.   And certainly on this head the Greeks, more than any people that ever lived, must have required a consolation and a hope.   Just in proportion as their life was fuller and richer than that which has been lived by any other race, just in proportion as their capacity for enjoyment, in body and soul, was keener, as their senses were finer, their intellect broader, their passions more intense, must they have felt, with peculiar emphasis, the horror of decay and death.   And such, in fact, is the characteristic note of their utterances on this theme. "Rather," says the ghost of Achilles to Odysseus in the world of shades, "rather would I live upon the soil as the hireling of another, with a landless man who had no great livelihood, than bear sway among all the dead that are no more." [1]   Better, as Shakespeare has it,

[1] Od. xi. 489.—Translated by Butcher and Lang

"The weariest and most loathed worldly life
    That age, ache, penury and imprisonment
    Can lay on nature,"

better that, on earth at least and in the sun, than the
phantom kingdoms of the dead. The fear of age
and death is the shadow of the love of life; and on
no people has it fallen with more horror than on the
Greeks. The tenderest of their songs of love close
with a sob; and it is an autumn wind that rustles in
their bowers of spring. Here, for example, is a
poem by Mimnermus characteristic of this mood of
the Greeks:

"O golden Love, what life, what joy but thine?
    Come death, when thou art gone, and make an end!
When gifts and tokens are no longer mine,
    Nor the sweet intimacies of a friend.
These are the flowers of youth. But painful age
    The bane of beauty, following swiftly on,
Wearies the heart of man with sad presage
    And takes away his pleasure in the sun.
Hateful is he to maiden and to boy
And fashioned by the gods for our annoy." [1]

Such being the general view of the Greeks on the
subject of death, what has their religion to say by
way of consolation? It taught, to begin with, that
the spirit does survive after death. But this survival, as it is described in the Homeric poems, is
merely that of a phantom and a shade, a bloodless
and colourless duplicate of the man as he lived "

[1] Mimnermus, El. 1.

earth.   Listen to the account Odysseus gives of his meeting with his mother's ghost.

"So spake she, and I mused in my heart and would fain have embraced the spirit of my mother dead. Thrice I sprang towards her, and was minded to embrace her; thrice she flitted from my hands as a shadow or even as a dream, and sharper ever waxed the grief within me.   And uttering my voice I spake to her winged words:

" 'Mother mine, wherefore dost thou not tarry for me who am eager to seize thee, that even in Hades we twain may cast our arms each about the other, and satisfy us with chill lament?   Is it but a phantom that the high goddess Persephone hath sent me, to the end that I may groan for more exceeding sorrow?'

"So spake I, and my lady mother answered me anon:

" 'Ah me, my child, luckless above all men, nought doth Persephone, the daughter of Zeus, deceive thee, but even in this wise it is with mortals when they die.   For the sinews no more bind together the flesh and the bones, but the force of burning fire abolishes them, so soon as the life hath left the white bones, and the spirit like a dream flies forth and hovers near.' " [1]

From such a conception of the life after death little comfort could be drawn; nor does it appear that any was sought.   So far as we can trace the habitual attitude of the Greek he seems to have occupied himself little with speculation, either for good or evil, as

[1] Od. xi. 204.—Translated by Butcher and Lang.

to what might await him on the other side of the
tomb.   He was told indeed in his legends of a happy
place for the souls of heroes, and of torments reserved for great criminals; but these ideas do not
seem to have haunted his imagination.   He was
never obsessed by that close and imminent vision of
heaven and hell which overshadowed and dwarfed,
for the mediæval mind, the brief space of pilgrimage
on earth.   Rather he turned, by preference, from the
thought of death back to life, and in the memory of
honourable deeds in the past and the hope of fame
for the future sought his compensation for the loss
of youth and love.   In the great funeral speech upon
those who have fallen in war which Thucydides puts
into the mouth of Pericles we have, we must suppose,
a reflection, more accurate than is to be found elsewhere, of the position naturally adopted by the average Greek.   And how simple are the topics, how
broad and human, how rigorously confined to the
limits of experience!   There is no suggestion anywhere of a personal existence continued after death;
the dead live only in their deeds; and only by memory are the survivors to be consoled.

"I do not now commiserate the parents of the
dead who stand here; I would rather comfort them.
You know that your life has been passed amid mani-
fold vicissitudes; and that they may be deemed fortunate who have gained most honour, whether an
honourable death like theirs, or an honourable sorrow like yours, and whose days have been so ordered
that the term of their happiness is likewise the term
of their life. . . . Some of you are at an age at which

they may hope to have other children, and they ought to bear their sorrow better; not only will the children who may hereafter be born make them forget their now lost ones, but the city will be doubly a gainer. She will not be left desolate, and she will be safer. For a man's counsels·cannot be of equal weight or worth, when he alone has no children to risk in the general danger. To those of you who have passed their prime, I say: 'Congratulate yourselves that you have been happy during the greater part of your days; remember that your life of sorrow will not last long, and be comforted by the glory of those who are gone. For the love of honour alone is ever young, and not riches, as some say, but honour is the delight of men when they are old and useless.' " [1]

The passage perhaps represents what we may call the typical attitude of the Greek. To seek consolation for death, if anywhere, then in life, and in life not as it might be imagined beyond the grave, but as it had been and would be lived on earth, appears to be consonant with all that we know of the clear and objective temper of the race. It is the spirit which was noted long ago by Goethe as inspiring the sepulchral monuments of Athens.

"The wind," he says, "which blows from the tombs of the ancients comes with gentle breath as over a mound of roses. The reliefs are touching and pathetic, and always represent life. There stand father and mother, their son between them, gazing at one another with unspeakable truth to nature.

[1] Thuc. II. 44.—Jowett's translation.

Here a pair clasp hands. Here a father seems to
rest on his couch and wait to be entertained by h᷾s
family. To me the presence of these scenes was
very touching. Their art is of a late period, yet are
they simple, natural, and of universal interest.
Here there is no knight in harness on his knees await-
ing a joyful resurrection. The artist has with more
or less skill presented to us only the persons themselves, and so made their existence lasting and perpetual. They fold not their hands, gaze not into
heaven; they are on earth, what they were and what
they are. They stand side by side, take interest in
one another; and that is what is in the stone, even
though somewhat unskilfully, yet most pleasingly depicted." [1]

As a further illustration of the same point an
epitaph may be quoted equally striking for its simple
human feeling and for its absence of any suggestion
of a continuance of the life of the dead. "Farewell"
is the first and last word; no hint of a "joyful resurrection."

"Farewell, tomb of Melité; the best of women
lies here, who loved her loving husband, Onesimus;
thou wert most excellent, wherefore he longs for thee
after thy death, for thou wert the best of wives.—
Farewell, thou too, dearest husband, only love my
children." [2]

[1] From Goethe's "Italienische Reise." I take this
translation (by permission) from Percy Gardner's "New
Chapters in Greek History," p. 319.
[2] Percy Gardner, "New Chapters in Greek History,"
p. 325.

But however characteristic this attitude of the Greeks may appear to be, especially by contrast with the Christian view, it would be a mistake to suppose that it was the only one with which they were acquainted, or that they had put aside altogether, as indifferent or insoluble, the whole problem of a future world. As we have seen, they did believe in the survival of the spirit, and in a world of shades ruled by Pluto and Persephone. They had legends of a place of bliss for the good and a place of torment for the wicked; and if this conception did not haunt their mind, as it haunted that of the mediæval Christian, yet at times it was certainly present to them, with terror or with hope. That the Greek was not unacquainted with the fear of hell we know from the passage of Plato, part of which we have already quoted, where in speaking of the mendicant prophets who professed to make atonement for sin he says that their ministrations "are equally at the service of the living and the dead; the latter sort they call mysteries, and they redeem us from the pains of hell, but if we neglect them no one knows what awaits us." [1]   And on the other hand we hear, as early as the date of the Odyssey, of the Elysian fields reserved for the souls of the favourites of the gods.

The Greeks, then, were not without hope and fear concerning the world to come, however little these feelings may have coloured their daily life; and there was one phase of their religion, which appears

---

[1] Plato, Rep. II. 364 e.—Jowett's translation.

to have been specially occupied with this theme. In almost every Greek city we hear of "mysteries," the most celebrated being, of course, those of Eleusis in Attica. What exactly these "mysteries" were we are very imperfectly informed; but so much, at least, is clear that by means of a scenic symbolism, representing the myth of Demeter and Kore or of Dionysus Zagreus, hopes were held out to the initiated not only of a happy life on earth, but of a happy immortality beyond. "Blessed," says Pindar, "blessed is he who has seen these things before he goes under the hollow earth. He knows the end of life, and he knows its god-given origin." And it is presumably to the initiated that the same poet promises the joys of his thoroughly Greek heaven. "For them," he says, "shineth below the strength of the sun while in our world it is night, and the space of crimson-flowered meadows before their city is full of the shade of frankincense-trees, and of fruits of gold. And some in horses, and in bodily feats, and some in dice, and some in harp-playing have delight; and among them thriveth all fair-flowering bliss; and fragrance streameth ever through the lovely land, as they mingle incense of every kind upon the altars of the gods." [1]

The Greeks, then, were not unfamiliar with the conception of heaven and hell; only, and that is the point to which we must return and on which we must insist, the conception did not dominate and obsess their mind. They may have had their spasms

[1] Pindar, Thren. I.—Translation by E. Myers.

of terror, but these they could easily relieve by the performance of some atoning ceremony; they may have had their thrills of hope, but these they would only indulge at the crisis of some imposing ritual. The general tenor of their life does not seem to have been much affected by speculations about the world beyond. Of age indeed and of death they had a horror proportional to their acute and sensitive enjoyment of life; but their natural impulse was to turn for consolation to the interests and achievements of the world they knew, and to endeavour to soothe, by memories and hopes of deeds future and past, the inevitable pains of failure and decay.

§ 12. Critical and Sceptical Opinion in Greece

And now let us turn to a point for which perhaps some readers have long been waiting, and with which they may have expected us to begin rather than to end. So far, in considering the part played by religion in Greek life, we have assumed the position of orthodoxy. We have endeavoured to place ourselves at the standpoint of the man who did not criticize or reflect, but accepted simply, as a matter of course, the tradition handed down to him by his fathers. Only so, if at all, was it possible for us to detach ourselves from our habitual preconceptions, and to regard the pagan mythology not as a graceful invention of the poets, but as a serious and, at the time, a natural and inevitable way of looking at the world. Now, however, it is time to turn to the other side, and to consider the Greek religion as it appeared to contemporary critics. For critics there were, and sceptics, or rather, to put it more exactly, there was a critical age succeeding an age of faith. As we trace, however imperfectly, the development of the Greek mind, we can observe their intellect and their moral sense expanding beyond the limits of their creed. Either as sympathetic, though candid, friends, or as avowed enemies, they bring to light its contradictions and defects; and as a result of the process one of two things happens. Either the ancient conception of the gods is transformed in the direction of monotheism, or it is altogether swept away, and a new system of the world built up, on the basis of natural science or of philosophy. These tendencies of thought we must now endeavour to trace; for we should have formed but an imperfect idea of the scope of the religious consciousness of the Greeks if we confined ourselves to what we may call their orthodox faith. It is in their most critical thinkers, in Euripides and Plato, that the religious sense is most fully and keenly developed; and it is in the philosophy that supervened upon the popular creed, rather than in the popular creed itself, that we shall find the highest and most spiritual reaches of their thought.

Let us endeavour, then, in the first place to realize to ourselves how the Greek religion must have appeared to one who approached it not from the side of unthinking acquiescence, but with the idea of discovering for himself how far it really met the needs and claims of the intellect and the moral sense. Let us imagine him turning to his Homer, to those poems which were almost the Bible of the Greek, his ultimate appeal both in religion and in ethics; which were taught in the schools, quoted in the law-courts, recited in the streets; and from which the teacher drew his moral instances, the rhetorician his allusions, the artist his models, every man his conception of the gods. Let us imagine some candid and ingenuous youth, turning to his Homer and repeating, say, the following passage of the Iliad:—

"Among the other gods fell grievous bitter strife, and their hearts were carried diverse in their breasts. And they clashed together with a great noise, and the wide earth groaned, and the clarion of great Heaven rang around. Zeus heard as he sate upon Olympus, and his heart within him laughed pleasantly when he beheld that strife of the gods." [1]

At this point, let us suppose, the reader pauses to reflect; and is struck, for the first time, with a shock of surprise by the fact that the gods should be not only many but opposed; and opposed on what issue? a purely human one! a war between Greeks and Trojans for the possession of a beautiful woman! Into such a contest the immortal gods descend, fight with human weapons, and dispute in human terms! Where is the single purpose that should mark the divine will? where the repose of the wisdom that foreordained and knows the end?   Not, it is clear,

[1] Iliad xxi. 385.—Translated by Lang, Leaf and Myers.

in this motley array of capricious and passionate
wills! Then, perhaps, in Zeus, Zeus, who is lord of
all? He, at least, will impose upon this mob of
recalcitrant deities the harmony which the pious soul
demands. He, whose rod shakes the sky, will arise
and assert the law. He, in his majesty, will speak
the words—alas! what words! Let us take them
straight from the lips of the King of gods and
men:—

"Hearken to me, all gods and all ye goddesses,
that I may tell you that my heart within my breast
commandeth me. One thing let none essay, be it
goddess or be it god, to wit, to thwart my saying;
approve ye it all altogether, that with all speed I
may accomplish these things. Whomsoever I shall
perceive minded to go, apart from the gods, to suc-
cour Trojans or Danaans, chastened in no seemly
wise shall he return to Olympus, or I will take and
cast him into misty Tartaros, right far away, where
is the deepest gulf beneath the earth; there are the
gate of iron and threshold of bronze, as far beneath
Hades as heaven is high above the earth: then shall
ye know how far I am mightiest of all gods. Go to
now, ye gods, make trial that ye all may know.
Fasten ye a rope of gold from heaven, and all ye
gods lay hold thereof and all goddesses; yet could
ye not drag from heaven to earth Zeus, counsellor
supreme, not though ye toiled sore. But once I likewise were minded to draw with all my heart, then
should I draw ye up with very earth and sea withal.
Thereafter would I bind the rope about a pinnacle
of Olympus, and so should all those things be hung

in air. By so much am I beyond gods and beyond men." [1]

And is that all? In the divine tug-of-war Zeus is more than a match for all the other gods together! Is it on this that the lordship of heaven and earth depends? This that we are to worship as highest, we of the brain and heart and soul? And even so, even admitting the ground of supremacy, with what providence or consistency of purpose is it exercised? Why, Zeus himself is as capricious as the rest! Because Thetis comes whining to him about an insult put upon Achilles, he interferes to change the whole course of the war, and that too by means of a lying dream! Even his own direct decrees he can hardly be induced to observe. His son Sarpedon, for example, who is "fated," as he says himself, to die, he is yet at the last moment in half a mind to save alive! How is such division possible in the will of the supreme god? Or is the "fate" of which he speaks something outside himself? But if so, then above him! and if above him, what is he? Not, after all, the highest, not the supreme at all! What then *are* we to worship? What *is* this higher "fate"?

Such would be the kind of questions that would vex our candid youth when he approached his Homer from the side of theology. Nor would he fare any better if he took the ethical point of view. The gods, he would find, who should surely at least attain to the human standard, not only are capable of every phase of passion, anger, fear, jealousy, and,

[1] Iliad. viii. 5.—Translated by Lang, Leaf and Myers.

above all, love, but indulge them all with a verve and an abandonment that might make the boldest libertine pause. Zeus himself, for example, expends upon the mere catalogue of his amours a good twelve lines of hexameter verse. No wonder that Hera is jealous, and that her lord is driven to put her down in terms better suited to the lips of mortal husbands:

"Lady, ever art thou imagining, nor can I escape thee; yet shalt thou in no wise have power to fulfil, but wilt thou be the further from my heart; that shall be even the worse for thee. Hide thou in silence and hearken to my bidding, lest all the gods that are in Olympus keep not off from thee my visitation, when I put forth my hands unapproachable against thee." [1]

§ 13. ETHICAL CRITICISM

The incongruity of all this with any adequate conception of deity is patent, if once the critical attitude be adopted; and it was adopted by some of the clearest and most religious minds of Greece. Nay, even orthodoxy itself did not refrain from a genial and sympathetic criticism. Aristophanes, for example, who, if there had been an established church, would certainly have been described as one of its main pillars, does not scruple to represent his Birds as issuing—

"A warning and notices, formally given,
To Jove, and all others residing in heaven,

---

[1] Iliad i. 560.—Translated by Leaf, Lang and Myers.

Forbidding them ever to venture again
To trespass on our atmospheric domain,
With scandalous journeys, to visit a list
Of Alcmenas and Semeles; if they persist,
We warn them that means will be taken moreover
To stop their gallanting and acting the lover."

and Heracles the glutton, and Dionysus, the dandy and the coward, are familiar figures of his comic stage.

The attitude of Aristophanes, it is true, is not really critical, but sympathetic; it was no more his intention to injure the popular creed by his fun than it is the intention of the cartoons of Punch to undermine the reputation of our leading statesmen. On the contrary, nothing popularizes like genial ridicule; and of this Aristophanes was well aware. But the same characteristics of the gods which suggested the friendly burlesque of the comedians were also those which provoked the indignation and the disgust of more serious minds. The poet Pindar, for example, after referring to the story of a battle, in which it was said gods had fought against gods, breaks out into protest against a legend so little creditable to the divine nature:—"O my mouth, fling this tale from thee, for to speak evil of gods is a hateful wisdom, and loud and unmeasured words strike a note that trembleth upon madness. Of such things talk thou not; leave war and all strife of immortals aside." [2]   And the same note is taken up

---

[1] Aristophanes, "Birds" 556.—Translation by Frere.
[2] Pind. Ol. IX. 54.—Translation by E. Myers.

with emphasis, and reiterated in every quality of tone, by such writers as Euripides and Plato.

The attitude of Euripides towards the popular religion is so clearly and frankly critical that a recent writer has even gone so far as to maintain that his main object in the construction of his dramas was to discredit the myths he selected for his theme. However that may have been, it is beyond controversy true that the deep religious sense of this most modern of the Greeks was puzzled and repelled by the tales he was bound by tradition to dramatize; and that he put into the mouth of his characters reflexions upon the conduct of the gods which if they may not be taken as his own deliberate opinions, are at least expressions of one aspect of his thought. It was, in fact, impossible to reconcile with a profound and philosophic view of the divine nature the intrigues and amours, partialities, antipathies, actions and counter-actions of these anthropomorphic deities. Consider, for example, the most famous of all the myths, that of Orestes, to which we have already referred. Orestes, it will be remembered, was the son of Agamemnon and Clytemnestra. Agamemnon, on his return from Troy, was murdered by Clytemnestra. Orestes escapes; but returns later, at the instigation of Apollo, and kills his mother to avenge his father. Thereupon, in punishment for his crime, he is persecuted by the Furies. Now the point which Euripides seizes here is the conduct of Apollo. Either it was right for Orestes to kill his mother, or it was wrong. If wrong, why did Apollo command it? If right, why was Orestes punished?

Or are there, as Æschylus would have it, two "rights," one of Apollo, the other of the Furies? If so, what becomes of that unity of the divine law after which every religious nature seeks? The dilemma is patent; and Euripides makes no serious attempt to meet it.

Or again, to take another example, less familiar, but even more to the point—the tale of Ion and Creusa. Creusa has been seduced by Apollo and has borne him a child, the Ion of the story. This child she exposes, and it is conveyed by Hermes to Delphi, where at last it is found, and recognized by the mother, and a conventionally happy ending is patched up. But the point on which the poet has insisted throughout is, once more, the conduct of Apollo. What is to be made of a god who seduces and deserts a mortal woman; who suffers her to expose her child, and leaves her in ignorance of its fate? Does he not deserve the reproaches heaped upon him by his victim?—

> "Child of Latona, I cry to the sun—I will publish
>   thy shame!
> Thou with thy tresses a-shimmer with gold, through
>   the flowers as I came
> Plucking the crocuses, heaping my veil with their
>   gold-litten flame,
> Cam'st on me, caughtest the poor pallid wrists of
>   mine hands, and didst hale
> Unto thy couch in the cave. 'Mother! mother!'
>   I shrieked out my wail—
> Wroughtest the pleasure of Kypris; no shame made
>   the god-lover quail.

Wretched I bare thee a child, and I cast him with
    shuddering throe
Forth on thy couch where thou forcedst thy victim,
    a bride-bed of woe.
Lost—my poor baby and thine! for the eagles
    devoured him: and lo!
Victory-songs to thy lyre dost thou chant!—Ho, I
    call to thee, son
Born to Latona, Dispenser of boding, on gold-
    gleaming throne
Midmost of earth who are sitting:—thine ears shall
    be pierced with my moan!
Thy Delos doth hate thee, thy bay-boughs abhor
    thee,
By the palm-tree of feathery frondage that rose
Where in sacred travail Latona bore thee
    In Zeus's garden close." [1]

This is a typical example of the kind of criticism
which Euripides conveys through the lips of his
characters on the stage.   And the points which he
can only dramatically suggest, Plato expounds directly in his own person.   The quarrel of the philosopher with the myths is not that they are not true,
but that they are not edifying.   They represent the
son in rebellion against the father—Zeus against
Kronos, Kronos against Uranos; they describe the
gods as intriguing and fighting one against the other;
they depict them as changing their form divine into
the semblance of mortal men; lastly—culmination
of horror!—they represent them as laughing, posi-
tively laughing!—Or again, to turn to a more meta-

[1] Euripid.   Ion. 885.—Translated by A. S. Way.

physical point, if God be good, it is argued by Plato, he cannot be the author of evil.   What then, are we to make of the passage in Homer where he says, "two urns stand upon the floor of Zeus filled with his evil gifts, and one with blessings.   To whomsoever Zeus whose joy is in the lightning dealeth a mingled lot, that man chanceth now upon ill and now again on good, but to whom he giveth but of the bad kind, him he bringeth to scorn, and evil famine chaseth him over the goodly earth, and he is a wanderer honoured of neither gods nor men." [1]

And again, if God be true, he cannot be the author of lies.   How then could he have sent, as we are told he did, lying dreams to men?—Clearly, concludes the philosopher, our current legends need revision; in the interest of religion itself we must destroy the myths of the popular creed.

§ 14. Transition to Monotheism

The myths, but not religion!   The criticism certainly of Plato and probably of Euripides was prompted by the desire not to discredit altogether the belief in the gods, but to bring it into harmony with the requirements of a more fully developed consciousness.   The philosopher and the poet came not to destroy, but to fulfil; not to annihilate, but to transform the popular theology.   Such an intention, strange as it may appear to us with our rigid creeds, we shall see to be natural enough to the Greek mind,

[1] Iliad xxiv. 527.—Translated by Lang, Leaf and Myers.

when we remember that the material of their religion was not a set of propositions, but a more or less indeterminate body of traditions capable of being presented in the most various forms as the genius and taste of individual poets might direct. And we find, in fact, that the most religious poets of Greece, those even who were most innocent of any intention to innovate on popular beliefs, did nevertheless unconsciously tend to transform, in accordance with their own conceptions, the whole structure of the Homeric theology. Taking over the legends of gods and heroes, as narrated in poetry and tradition, Æschylus and Sophocles, as they shaped and reshaped their material for the stage, were evolving for themselves, not in opposition to but as it were on the top of the polytheistic view, the idea of a single supreme and righteous God. The Zeus of Homer, whose superiority, as we saw, was based on physical force, grows, under the hands of Æschylus, into something akin to the Jewish Jehovah. The inner experience of the poet drives him inevitably to this transformation. Born into the great age of Greece, coming to maturity at the crisis of her fate, he had witnessed with his own eyes, and assisted with his own hands the defeat of the Persian host at Marathon. The event struck home to him like a judgment from heaven. The Nemesis that attends upon human pride, the vengeance that follows crime, henceforth were the thoughts that haunted and possessed his brain; and under their influence he evolved for himself out of the popular idea of Zeus the conception of a God of justice who marks and

avenges crime. Read for example the following
passage from the "Agamemnon" and contrast it with
the lines of Homer quoted on page 42. Nothing
could illustrate more strikingly the transformation
that could be effected, under the conditions of the
Greek religion, in the whole conception of the divine power by one whose conscious intention, nevertheless, was not to innovate but to conserve.

"Zeus the high God! whate'er be dim in doubt,
          This can our thought track out—
The blow that fells the sinner is of God,
          And as he wills, the rod
Of vengeance smiteth sore.   One said of old
          'The gods list not to hold
A reckoning with him whose feet oppress
          The grace of holiness'—
An impious word! for whensoe'er the sire
          Breathed forth rebellious fire—
What time his household overflows the measure
          Of bliss and health and treasure—
His children's children read the reckoning plain,
          At last, in tears and pain.
          *   *   *   *   *
Who spurns the shrine of Right, nor wealth nor power
          Shall be to him a tower,
To guard him from the gulf: there lies his lot,
          Where all things are forgot.
Lust drives him on—lust, desperate and wild
          Fate's sin-contriving child—
And cure is none; beyond concealment clear
          Kindles sin's baleful glare.
As an ill coin beneath the wearing touch
          Betrays by stain and smutch

> Its metal false—such is the sinful wight.
>> Before, on pinions light,
> Fair pleasure flits, and lures him childlike on,
>> While home and kin make moan
> Beneath the grinding burden of his crime;
>> Till, in the end of time,
> Cast down of heaven, he pours forth fruitless prayer
> To powers that will not hear." [1]

And Sophocles follows in the same path. For him too Zeus is no longer the god of physical strength: he is the creator and sustainer of the moral law—of "those laws of range sublime, called into life throughout the high clear heaven, whose father is Olympus alone; their parent was no race of mortal men, no, nor shall oblivion ever lay them to sleep; a mighty god is in them, and he grows not old." [2] Such words imply a complete transformation of the Homeric conception of Divinity; a transformation made indeed in the interests of religion, but involving nevertheless, and contrary, no doubt, to the intentions of its authors, a complete subversion of the popular creed. Once grant the idea of God as an eternal and moral Power and the whole fabric of polytheism falls away. The religion of the Greeks, as interpreted by their best minds, annihilates itself. Zeus indeed is saved, but only at the cost of all Olympus.

[1] Æsch. Agamem. 367.—Translated by E. D. A. Morshead ("The House of Atreus").
[2] Soph. O. T. 865.—Translated by Dr. Jebb.

§ 15. METAPHYSICAL CRITICISM

While thus, on the one hand, the Greek religion by its inner evolution was tending to destroy itself, on the other hand it was threatened from without by the attack of what we should call the "scientific spirit." A system so frankly anthropomorphic was bound to be weak on the speculative side. Its appeal, as we have seen, was rather to the imagination than to the intellect, by the presentation of a series of beautiful images, whose contemplation might offer to the mind if not satisfaction, at least acquiescence and repose. A Greek who was not too inquisitive was thus enabled to move through the calendar of splendid festivals and fasts, charmed by the beauty of the ritual, inspired by the chorus and the dance, and drawing from the familiar legends the moral and æsthetic significance with which he had been accustomed from his boyhood to connect them, but without ever raising the question, Is all this true? Does it really account for the existence and nature of the world? Once, however, the spell was broken, once the intellect was aroused, the inadequacy of the popular faith, on the speculative side, became apparent; and the mind turned aside altogether from religion to work out its problems on its own lines. We find accordingly, from early times, physical philosophers in Greece free from all theological preconceptions, raising from the very beginning the question of the origin of the world, and offering solutions, various indeed but all alike in this, that they frankly accept a materialistic basis. One derives all things from water, another from air, another from fire; one insists upon unity, another on a plurality of elements, but all alike reject the supernatural, and proceed on the lines of physical causation.

The opposition, to use the modern phrase, between science and religion, was thus developed early in ancient Greece; and by the fifth century it is clear that it had become acute. The philosopher Anaxagoras was driven from Athens as an atheist; the same charge, absurdly enough, was one of the counts in the indictment of Socrates; and the physical speculations of the time are a favourite butt of that champion of orthodoxy, Aristophanes. To follow up these speculations in detail would be to wander too far from our present purpose; but it may be worth while to quote a passage from the great comedian, to illustrate not indeed the value of the theories ridiculed, but their generally materialistic character, and their antagonism to the popular faith. The passage selected is part of a dialogue between Socrates and Strepsiades, one of his pupils; and it is introduced by an address from the chorus of "Clouds," the new divinities of the physicist:

CHORUS OF CLOUDS.
  Our welcome to thee, old man, who would see the marvels that science can show:
  And thou, the high-priest of this subtlety feast, say what would you have us bestow?
  Since there is not a sage for whom we'd engage our wonders more freely to do,

Except, it may be, for Prodicus: he for his knowledge
    may claim them, but you,
Because, as you go, you glance to and fro, and in dig-
    nified arrogance float;
And think shoes a disgrace, and put on a grave face,
    your acquaintance with us to denote.

STREPSIADES.

Oh, earth! what a sound, how august and profound! it
    fills me with wonder and awe.

SOCRATES.

These, these then alone, for true Deities own, the rest
    are all God-ships of straw.

STREPS.

Let Zeus be left out: He's a God beyond doubt; come,
    that you can scarcely deny.

SOCR.

Zeus indeed! there's no Zeus: don't you be so obtuse.

STREPS.

No Zeus up above in the sky?
Then you first must explain, who it is sends the rain;
    or I really must think you are wrong.

SOCR.

Well then, be it known, these send it alone: I can prove
    it by argument strong.
Was there ever a shower seen to fall in an hour when
    the sky was all cloudless and blue?
Yet on a fine day, when the clouds are away, he might
    send one, according to you.

STREPS.

Well, it must be confessed, that chimes in with the rest:
    your words I am forced to believe.
Yet before I had dreamed that the rain-water steamed
    from Zeus and his chamber-pot sieve.
But whence then, my friend, does the thunder descend?
    that does make us quake with affright!

SOCR.

Why, 'tis they, I declare, as they roll through the air.

STREPS.

What the clouds? did I hear you aright?

SOCR.

Ay: for when to the brim filled with water they swim,
by Necessity carried along,

They are hung up on high in the vault of the sky, and
so by Necessity strong

In the midst of their course, they clash with great force,
and thunder away without end.

STREPS.

But is it not He who compels this to be? does not Zeus
this Necessity send?

SOCR.

No Zeus have we there, but a vortex of air.

STREPS.

What! Vortex? that's something I own.

I knew not before, that Zeus was no more, but Vortex
was placed on his throne!

But I have not yet heard to what cause you referred the
thunder's majestical roar.

SOCR.

Yes, 'tis they, when on high full of water they fly, and
then, as I told you before,

By compression impelled, as they clash, are compelled
a terrible clatter to make.

STREPS.

Come, how can that be?   I really don't see.

SOCR.

Yourself as my proof I will take.

Have you never then ate the broth puddings you get
when the Panathenaea come round,

And felt with what might your bowels all night in tur-
bulent tumult resound?

STREPS.

> By Apollo, 'tis true, there's a mighty to do, and my belly
> keeps rumbling about;
> And the puddings begin to clatter within and to kick up
> a wonderful rout:
> Quite gently at first, papapax, papapax, but soon pap-
> appappax away,
> Till at last, I'll be bound, I can thunder as loud pap-
> apappappappappax as they.

SOCR.

> Shalt thou then a sound so loud and profound from thy
> belly diminutive send,
> And shall not the high and the infinite sky go thunder-
> ing on without end?
> For both, you will find, on an impulse of wind and
> similar causes depend.

STREPS.

> Well, but tell me from whom comes the bolt through the
> gloom, with its awful and terrible flashes;
> And wherever it turns, some it singes and burns, and
> some it reduces to ashes:
> For this 'tis quite plain, let who will send the rain, that
> Zeus against perjurers dashes.

SOCR.

> And how, you old fool, of a dark-ages school, and an
> antediluvian wit,
> If the perjured they strike, and not all men alike, have
> they never Cleonymus hit?
> Then of Simon again, and Theorus explain: known
> perjurers, yet they escape.
> But he smites his own shrine with these arrows divine,
> and "Sunium, Attica's cape,"
> And the ancient gnarled oaks: now what prompted
> those strokes? They never forswore I should
> say.

STREPS.

    Can't say that they do: your words appear true.
      Whence comes then the thunderbolt, pray?

SOCR.

    When a wind that is dry, being lifted on high, is sud-
      denly pent into these,
    It swells up their skin, like a bladder, within, by Ne-
      cessity's changeless decrees.
    Till compressed very tight, it bursts them outright, and
      away with an impulse so strong,
    That at last by the force and the swing of the course, it
      takes fire as it whizzes along.

STREPS.

    That's exactly the thing, that I suffered one spring, at
      the great feast of Zeus, I admit:
    I'd a paunch in the pot, but I wholly forgot about mak-
      ing the safety-valve slit.
    So it spluttered and swelled, while the saucepan I held,
      till at last with a vengeance it flew:
    Took me quite by surprise, dung-bespattered my eyes,
      and scalded my face black and blue! [1]

Nothing could be more amusing than this passage
as a burlesque of the physical theories of the
time; and nothing could better illustrate the quarrel
between science and religion, as it presents itself
on the surface to the plain man. But there is
more in the quarrel than appears at first sight.
The real sting of the comedy from which we have
quoted lies in the assumption, adopted throughout
the play, that the atheist is also necessarily anti-
social and immoral. The physicist, in the person

[1] Aristoph. "Clouds" 358.—Translated by B. B.
Rogers.

of Socrates, is identified with the sophist; on the one hand he is represented as teaching the theory of material causation, on the other the art of lying and deceit. The object of Strepsiades in attending the school is to learn how not to pay his debts; the achievement of his son is to learn how to dishonour his father. The cult of reason is identified by the poet with the cult of self-interest; the man who does not believe in the gods cannot, he implies, believe in the family or the state.

§ 16. METAPHYSICAL RECONSTRUCTION—PLATO

The argument is an old one into whose merits this is not the place to enter. But one thing is certain, that the sceptical spirit which was invading religion, was invading also politics and ethics; and that towards the close of the fifth century before Christ, Greece and in particular Athens was overrun by philosophers, who not only did not scruple to question the foundations of social and moral obligation, but in some cases explicitly taught that there were no foundations at all; that all law was a convention based on no objective truth; and that the only valid right was the natural right of the strong to rule. It was into this chaos of sceptical opinion that Plato was born; and it was the desire to meet and subdue it that was the motive of his philosophy. Like Aristophanes, he traced the root of the evil to the decay of religious belief; and though no one, as we have seen, was more trenchant than he in his criticism of the popular faith, no one, on the other hand, was more convinced of the necessity of some form of religion as a basis for any stable polity. The doctrine of the physicists, he asserts, that the world is the result of "nature and chance" has immediate and disastrous effects on the whole structure of social beliefs. The conclusion inevitably follows that human laws and institutions, like everything else, are accidental products; that they have no objective validity, no binding force on the will, and that the only right that has any intelligible meaning is the right which is identical with might.[1] Against these conclusions the whole soul of Plato rose in revolt. To reconstruct religion, he was driven back upon metaphysics; and elaborated at last the system which from his day to our own has not ceased to perplex and fascinate the world, and whose rare and radiant combination of gifts, speculative, artistic, and religious, marks the highest reach of the genius of the Greeks, and perhaps of mankind.

To attempt an analysis of that system would lead us far from our present task. All that concerns us here, is its religious significance; and of that, all we can note is that Plato, the deepest thinker of the Greeks, was also among the farthest removed from the popular faith. The principle from which he derives the World is the absolute Good, or God, of whose ideas the phenomena of sense are imperfect copies. To the divine intelligence man by virtue of his reason is akin. But the reason in him has fallen

---

[1] See *e.g.* Plato's "Laws" x. 887.

into bondage of the flesh; and it is the task of his
life on earth, or rather of a series of lives (for Plato
believed in successive re-incarnations), to deliver
this diviner element of his soul, and set it free to re-
unite with God.   To the description of the divine
life thus prepared for the soul, from which she fell
but to which she may return, Plato has devoted some
of his finest passages; and if we are to indicate, as
we are bound to do, the highest point to which the
religious consciousness of the Greeks attained, we
must not be deterred, by dread of the obscurity necessarily attaching to an extract, from a citation
from the most impassioned of his dialogues.   Speaking of that "divine madness," to which we have already had occasion to refer, he says that this is the
madness which "is imputed to him who, when he
sees the beauty of earth, is transported with the rec-
ollection of true beauty; he would like to fly away,
but he cannot; he is like a bird fluttering and looking upward and careless of the world below; and he
is therefore thought to be mad.   And I have shown
this of all inspirations to be the noblest and highest
and the offspring of the highest to him who has or
shares in it, and that he who loves the beautiful is
called a lover because he partakes of it.   For every
soul of man has in the way of nature beheld true
being; this was the condition of her passing into the
form of man.   But all souls do not easily recall the
things of the other world; they may have seen them
for a short time only, or they may have been unfortunate in their earthly lot, and having had their
hearts turned to unrighteousness through some cor-

rupting influence, they may have lost the memory
of the holy things which once they saw. Few only
retain an adequate remembrance of them; and they,
when they behold here any image of that other
world, are rapt in amazement; but they are ignorant
of what that rapture means, because they do not
clearly perceive. For there is no clear light of justice or temperance, or any of the higher ideas which
are precious to souls, in the earthly copies of them;
they are seen through a glass dimly; and there are
few who, going to the images, behold in them the
realities, and these only with difficulty. There was
a time when, with the rest of the happy band, they
saw beauty shining in brightness—we philosophers
following in the train of Zeus, others in company
with other gods; and then we beheld the beatific
vision and were initiated into a mystery which may
be truly called most blessed, celebrated by us in our
state of innocence, before we had any experience of
evils to come, when we were admitted to the sight of
apparitions innocent and simple and calm and happy,
which we beheld shining in pure light, pure ourselves
and not yet enshrined in that living tomb which we
carry about, now that we are imprisoned in the body,
like an oyster in his shell. Let me linger over the
memory of scenes which have passed away." [1]

§ 17. SUMMARY

At this point, where religion passes into philosophy, the discussion which has occupied the present

[1] Plato, Phaedrus. 249 d.—Jowett's translation.

chapter must close. So far it was necessary to proceed, in order to show how wide was the range of the religious consciousness of the Greeks, and through how many points of view it passed in the course of its evolution. But its development was away from the Greek and towards the Christian; and it will therefore be desirable, in conclusion, to fix once more in our minds that central and primary phase of the Greek religion under the influence of which their civilization was formed into a character definite and distinct in the history of the world. This phase will be the one which underlay and was reflected in the actual cult and institutions of Greece, and must therefore be regarded not as a product of critical and self-conscious thought, but as an imaginative way of conceiving the world stamped, as it were, passively on the mind by the whole course of concrete experience. Of its character we have attempted to give some kind of account in the earlier part of this chapter, and we have now only to summarize what was there said.

The Greek religion, then, as we saw, in this its characteristic phase, involved a belief in a number of deities who on the one hand were personifications of the powers of nature and of the human soul, on the other the founders and sustainers of civil society. To the operations of these beings the whole of experience was referred, and that, not merely in an abstract and unintelligible way, as when we say that the world was created by God, but in a more precise and definite sense, the actions of the gods being conceived to be the same in kind as that of man, proceeding from similar motives, directed to similar ends, and accomplished very largely by similar, though much superior means. By virtue of this uncritical and unreflective mode of apprehension the Greeks, we said, were made at home in the world. Their religion suffused and transformed the facts both of nature and of society, interpreting what would otherwise have been unintelligible by the idea of an activity which they could understand because it was one which they were constantly exercising themselves. Being thus supplied with a general explanation of the world, they could put aside the question of its origin and end, and devote themselves freely and fully to the art of living, unhampered by scruples and doubts as to the nature of life. Consciousness similar to their own was the ultimate fact; and there was nothing therefore with which they might not form intelligible and harmonious relations.

And as on the side of metaphysics they were delivered from the perplexities of speculation, so on the side of ethics they were undisturbed by the perplexities of conscience. Their religion, it is true, had a bearing on their conduct, but a bearing, as we saw, external and mechanical. If they sinned they might be punished directly by physical evil; and from this evil religion might redeem them by the appropriate ceremonies of purgation. But on the other hand they were not conscious of a spiritual relation to God, of sin as an alienation from the divine power and repentance as the means of restoration to grace. The pang of conscience, the fears and hopes, the triumph and despair of the soul which were the preoccupations of the Puritan, were phenomena unknown to the ancient Greek. He lived and acted undisturbed by scrupulous introspection; and the function of his religion was rather to quiet the conscience by ritual than to excite it by admonition and reproof.

From both these points of view, the metaphysical and the ethical, the Greeks were brought by their religion into harmony with the world. Neither the perplexities of the intellect nor the scruples of the conscience intervened to hamper their free activity. Their life was simple, straightforward, and clear; and their consciousness directed outwards upon the world, not perplexedly absorbed in the contemplation of itself.

On the other hand, this harmony, which was the essence of the Greek civilization, was a temporary compromise, not a final solution. It depended on presumptions of the imagination, not on convictions of the intellect; and as we have seen, it destroyed itself by the process of its own development. The beauty, the singleness, and the freedom which attracts us in the consciousness of the Greek was the result of a poetical view of the world, which did but anticipate in imagination an ideal that was not realized in fact or in thought. It depended on the assumption of anthropomorphic gods, an assumption which could not stand before the criticism of reason, and either broke down into scepticism, or was developed into the conception of a single supreme and spiritual power.

And even apart from this internal evolution, from

this subversion of its ideal basis, the harmony established by the Greek religion was at the best but partial and incomplete. It was a harmony for life, but not for death. The more completely the Greek felt himself to be at home in the world, the more happily and freely he abandoned himself to the exercise of his powers, the more intensely and vividly he lived in action and in passion, the more alien, bitter, and incomprehensible did he find the phenomena of age and death. On this problem, so far as we can judge, he received from his religion but little light, and still less consolation. The music of his brief life closed with a discord unresolved; and even before reason had brought her criticism to bear upon his creed, its deficiency was forced upon him by his feeling.

Thus the harmony which we have indicated as the characteristic result of the Greek religion contained none of the conditions of completeness or finality. For on the one hand there were elements which it was never able to include; and on the other, its hold even over those which it embraced was temporary and precarious. The eating of the tree of knowledge drove the Greeks from their paradise; but the vision of that Eden continues to haunt the mind of man, not in vain, if it prophesies in a type the end to which his history moves.

CHAPTER II

§ 1. THE GREEK STATE A "CITY"

THE present kingdom of Greece is among the smallest of European states; but to the Greeks it would have appeared too large to be a state at all. Within that little peninsula whose whole population and wealth are so insignificant according to modern ideas, were comprised in classical times not one but many flourishing polities. And the conception of an amalgamation of these under a single government was so foreign to the Greek idea, that even to Aristotle, the clearest and most comprehensive thinker of his age, it did not present itself even as a dream. To him, as to every ancient Greek, the state meant the City—meant, that is to say, an area about the size of an English county, with a population, perhaps, of some hundred thousand, self-governing and independent of any larger political whole.

If we can imagine the various County Councils of England emancipated from the control of Parliament and set free to make their own laws, manage their own finances and justice, raise troops and form with one another alliances, offensive and defensive, we may form thus some general idea of the political institutions of the Greeks and some measure of their difference from our own.

Nor must it be supposed that the size of the Greek state was a mere accident in its constitution, that it might have been indefinitely enlarged and yet retained its essential character. On the contrary, the limitation of size belonged to its very notion. The greatest state, says Aristotle, is not the one whose population is most numerous; on the contrary, after a certain limit of increase has been passed, the state ceases to be a state at all. "Ten men are too few for a city; a hundred thousand are too many." Not only London, it seems, but every one of our larger towns, would have been too big for the Greek idea of a state; and as for the British empire, the very conception of it would have been impossible to the Greeks.

Clearly, their view on this point is fundamentally different from our own. Their civilization was one of "city-states," not of kingdoms and empires; and their whole political outlook was necessarily determined by this condition. Generalizing from their own experience, they had formed for themselves a conception of the state not the less interesting to us that it is unfamiliar; and this conception it will be the business of the present chapter to illustrate and explain.

§ 2. THE RELATION OF THE STATE TO THE CITIZEN

First, let us consider the relation of the state to the citizens—that is to say, to that portion of the

community, usually a minority, which was possessed
of full political rights.   It is here that we have the
key to that limitation of size which we have seen to
be essential to the idea of the city-state.   For, in
the Greek view, to be a citizen of a state did not
merely imply the payment of taxes, and the possession of a vote; it implied a direct and active co-
operation in all the functions of civil and military
life.   A citizen was normally a soldier, a judge, and
a member of the governing assembly; and all his
public duties he performed not by deputy, but in
person.   He must be able frequently to attend the
centre of government; hence the limitation of territory.   He must be able to speak and vote in person
in the assembly; hence the limitation of numbers.
The idea of representative government never occurred to the Greeks; but if it had occurred to them,
and if they had adopted it, it would have involved
a revolution in their whole conception of the citizen.
Of that conception, direct personal service was the
cardinal point—service in the field as well as in the
council; and to substitute for personal service the
mere right to a vote would have been to destroy the
form of the Greek state.

Such being the idea the Greeks had formed, based
on their own experience, of the relation of the citizen
to the state, it follows that to them a society so
complex as our own would hardly have answered to
the definition of a state at all.   Rather they would
have regarded it as a mere congeries of unsatisfac-
tory human beings, held together, partly by political,
partly by economic compulsion, but lacking that

conscious identity of interest with the community to which they belong which alone constitutes the citizen. A man whose main pre-occupation should be with his trade or his profession, and who should only become aware of his corporate relations when called upon for his rates and taxes—a man, that is to say, in the position of an ordinary Englishman— would not have seemed to the Greeks to be a full and proper member of a state. For the state, to them, was more than a machinery, it was a spiritual bond; and "public life," as we call it, was not a thing to be taken up and laid aside at pleasure, but a necessary and essential phase of the existence of a complete man.

This relation of the citizen to the state, as it was conceived by the Greeks, is sometimes described as though it involved the sacrifice of the individual to the whole. And in a certain sense, perhaps, this is true. Aristotle, for instance, declares that no one must suppose he belongs to himself, but rather that all alike belong to the state; and Plato, in the construction of his ideal republic, is thinking much less of the happiness of the individual citizens, than of the symmetry and beauty of the whole as it might appear to a disinterested observer from without. Certainly it would have been tedious and irksome to any but his own ideal philosopher to live under the rule of that perfect polity. Individual enterprise, bent, and choice is rigorously excluded. Nothing escapes the net of legislation, from the production of children to the fashion of houses, clothes, and food. It is absurd, says the ruthless logic of this mathema-

tician among the poets, for one who would regulate
public life to leave private relations uncontrolled; if
there is to be order at all, it must extend through
and through; no moment, no detail must be with-
drawn from the grasp of law.   And though in this,
Plato, no doubt, goes far beyond the common sense
of the Greeks, yet he is not building altogether in
the air.   The republic which he desiderates was
realized, as we shall see, partially at least, in Sparta.
So that his insistence on the all-pervading domina-
tion of the state, exaggerated though it be, is exaggerated on the actual lines of Greek practice, and
may be taken as indicative of a real distinction and
even antithesis between their point of view and that
which prevails at present in most modern states.

But on the other hand such a phrase as the "sacrifice of the individual to the whole," to this extent at
least is misleading, that it presupposes an opposition
between the end of the individual and that of the
State, such as was entirely foreign to the Greek conception.   The best individual, in their view, was also
the best citizen; the two ideals not only were not
incompatible, they were almost indistinguishable.
When Aristotle defines a state as "an association of
similar persons for the attainment of the best life
possible," he implies not only that society is the
means whereby the individual attains his ideal, but
also that that ideal includes the functions of public
life.   The state in his view is not merely the convenient machinery that raises a man above his animal wants and sets him free to follow his own devices; it is itself his end, or at least a part of it.

And from this it follows that the regulations of the state were not regarded by the Greeks—as they are apt to be by modern men—as so many vexatious, if necessary, restraints on individual liberty; but rather as the expression of the best and highest nature of the citizen, as the formula of the conduct which the good man would naturally prescribe to himself. So that, to get a clear conception of what was at least the Greek ideal, however imperfectly it may have been attained in practice, we ought to regard the individual not as sacrificed to, but rather as realizing himself in the whole. We shall thus come nearer to what seems to have been the point of view not only of Aristotle and of Plato, but also of the average Greek man.

§ 3. The Greek View of Law

For nothing is more remarkable in the political theory of the Greeks than the respect they habitually express for law. Early legislators were believed to have been specially inspired by the divine power— Lycurgus, for instance, by Apollo, and Minos by Zeus; and Plato regards it as a fundamental condition of the well-being of any state that this view should prevail among its citizens. Nor was this conception of the divine origin of law confined to legend and to philosophy; we find it expressed in the following passage of Demosthenes, addressed to a jury of average Athenians, and representing at any rate the conventional and orthodox, if not the critical view of the Greek public:

"The whole life of men, O Athenians, whether they inhabit a great city or a small one, is governed by nature and by laws. Of these, nature is a thing irregular, unequal, and peculiar to the individual possessor; laws are regular, common, and the same for all. Nature, if it be depraved, has often vicious desires; therefore you will find people of that sort falling into error. Laws desire what is just and honourable and useful; they seek for this, and, when it is found, it is set forth as a general ordinance, the same and alike for all; and that is law, which all men ought to obey for many reasons, and especially because every law is an invention and gift of the Gods, a resolution of wise men, a corrective of errors intentional and unintentional, a compact of the whole state, according to which all who belong to the state ought to live." [1]

In this opposition of Law, as the universal principle, to Nature, as individual caprice, is implied a tacit identification of Law and Justice. The identification, of course, is never complete in any state, and frequently enough is not even approximate. No people were more conscious of this than the Greeks, none, as we shall see later, pushed it more vigorously home. But still, the positive conception which lay at the root of their society was that which finds expression in the passage we have quoted, and which is stated still more explicitly in the "Memorabilia" of Xenophon, where that admirable example of the good and efficient citizen represents his hero Socrates

[1] Demosth. in Aristogeit. § 17.—Translation by C. R. Kennedy.

as maintaining, without hesitation or reserve, that "that which is in accordance with law is just." The implication, of course, is not that laws cannot be improved, that they do at any point adequately correspond to justice; but that justice has an objective and binding validity, and that Law is a serious and on the whole a successful attempt to embody it in practice. This was the conviction predominant in the best period of Greece; the conviction under which her institutions were formed and flourished, and whose overthrow by the philosophy of a critical age was coincident with, if it was not the cause of, her decline.

§ 4. Artisans and Slaves

We have now arrived at a general idea of the nature of the Greek state, and of its relations to the individual citizen. But there were also members of the state who were not citizens at all; there was the class of labourers and traders, who, in some states at least, had no political rights; and the class of slaves who had nowhere any rights at all. For in the Greek conception the citizen was an aristocrat. His excellence was thought to consist in public activity; and to the performance of public duties he ought therefore to be able to devote the greater part of his time and energy. But the existence of such a privileged class involved the existence of a class of producers to support them; and the producers, by the nature of their calling, be they slave or free, were excluded from the life of the perfect citizen. They had not the necessary leisure to devote to public business; neither had they the opportunity to acquire the mental and physical qualities which would enable them to transact it worthily. They were therefore regarded by the Greeks as an inferior class; in some states, in Sparta, for example, and in Thebes, they were excluded from political rights; and even in Athens, the most democratic of all the Greek communities, though they were admitted to the citizenship and enjoyed considerable political influence, they never appear to have lost the stigma of social inferiority. And the distinction which was thus more or less definitely drawn in practice between the citizens proper and the productive class, was even more emphatically affirmed in theory. Aristotle, the most balanced of all the Greek thinkers and the best exponent of the normal trend of their ideas, excludes the class of artisans from the citizenship of his ideal state on the ground that they are debarred by their occupation from the characteristic excellence of man. And Plato, though here as elsewhere he pushes the normal view to excess, yet, in his insistence on the gulf that separates the citizen from the mechanic and the trader, is in sympathy with the general current of Greek ideas. His ideal state is one which depends mainly on agriculture; in which commerce and exchange are reduced to the smallest possible dimensions; in which every citizen is a landowner, forbidden to engage in trade; and in which the productive class is excluded from all political rights.

The obverse, then, of the Greek citizen, who

realized in the state his highest life, was an inferior class of producers who realized only the means of subsistence. But within this class again was a distinction yet more fundamental—the distinction between free men and slaves. In the majority of the Greek states the slaves were the greater part of the population; in Athens, to take an extreme case, at the close of the fourth century, they are estimated at 400,000 to 100,000 citizens. They were employed not only in domestic service, but on the fields, in factories and in mines, and performed, in short, a considerable part of the productive labour in the state. A whole large section, then, of the producers in ancient Greece had no social or political rights at all. They existed simply to maintain the aristocracy of citizens, for whom and in whom the state had its being. Nor was this state of things in the least repugnant to the average Greek mind. Nothing is more curious to the modern man than the temper in which Aristotle approaches this theme. Without surprise or indignation, but in the tone of an impartial, scientific inquirer, he asks himself the question whether slavery is natural, and answers it in the affirmative. For, he argues, though in any particular case, owing to the uncertain chances of fortune and war, the wrong person may happen to be enslaved, yet, broadly speaking, the general truth remains, that there are some men so inferior to others that they ought to be despotically governed, by the same right and for the same good end that the body ought to be governed by the soul. Such men, he maintains, are slaves by nature; and it is as much

to their interest to be ruled as it is to their masters'
interest to rule them.   To this class belong, for example, all who are naturally incapable of any but
physical activity.   These should be regarded as de-
tachable limbs, so to speak, of the man who owns
them, instruments of his will, like hands and feet;
or, to use Aristotle's own phase, "the slave is a tool
with life in it, and the tool a lifeless slave."

The relation between master and slave thus
frankly conceived by the Greeks, did not necessarily
imply, though it was quite compatible with, brutality
of treatment.   The slave might be badly treated, no
doubt, and very frequently was, for his master had
almost absolute control over him, life and limb; but,
as we should expect, it was clearly recognized by
the best Greeks that the treatment should be genial
and humane.   "There is a certain mutual profit and
kindness," says Aristotle, "between master and slave,
in all cases where the relation is natural, not merely
imposed from without by convention or force." [1]
And Plato insists on the duty of neither insulting
nor outraging a slave, but treating him rather with
even greater fairness than if he were in a position of
equality.

Still, there can be no doubt that the Greek conception of slavery is one of the points in which their
view of life runs most counter to our own.   Centuries of Christianity have engendered in us the conviction, or, rather, the instinct, that men are equal at
least to this extent, that no one has a right explicitly

---

[1] Arist. Pol. I. 7. 1255 b 12.

to make of another a mere passive instrument of his will—that every man, in short, must be regarded as an end in himself.   Yet even here the divergence between the Greek and the modern view is less extreme than it appears at first sight.   For the modern man, in spite of his perfectly genuine belief in equality (in the sense in which we have just defined the word), does, nevertheless, when he is confronted with racial differences, recognize degrees of inferiority so extreme, that he is practically driven into the Aristotelian position that some men are naturally slaves. The American, for example, will hardly deny that such is his attitude towards the negro.   The negro, in theory, is the equal, politically and socially, of the white man; in practice, he is excluded from the vote, from the professions, from the amenities of social intercourse, and even, as we have recently learnt, from the most elementary forms of justice. The general and *à priori* doctrine of equality is shattering itself against the actual facts; and the old Greek conception, "the slave by nature," may be detected behind the mask of the Christian ideal.   And while thus, even in spite of itself, the modern view is approximating to that of the Greeks, on the other hand the Greek view by its own evolution was already beginning to anticipate our own.   Even Aristotle, in formulating his own conception of slavery, finds it necessary to observe that though it be true that some men are naturally slaves, yet in practice, under conditions which give the victory to force, it may happen that the "natural" slave becomes the master, and the "natural" master is degraded to a slave. This is already a serious modification of his doctrine. And other writers, pushing the contention further, deny altogether the theory of natural slavery. "No man," says the poet Philemon, "was ever born a slave by nature. Fortune only has put men in that position." And Euripides, the most modern of the Greeks, writes in the same strain: "One thing only disgraces a slave, and that is the name. In all other respects a slave, if he be good, is no worse than a freeman." [1]

It seems then that the distinction between the Greek and the modern point of view is not so profound or so final as it appears at first sight. Still, the distinction, broadly speaking, is there. The Greeks, on the whole, were quite content to sacrifice the majority to the minority. Their position, as we said at the outset, was fundamentally aristocratic; they exaggerated rather than minimized the distinctions between men—between the Greek and the barbarian, the freeman and the slave, the gentleman and the artisan—regarding them as natural and fundamental, not as the casual product of circumstances. The "equality" which they sought in a well-ordered state was proportional not arithmetical—the attribution to each of his peculiar right, not of equal rights to all. Some were born to rule, others to serve; some to be ends, others to be means; and the problem to be solved was not how to obliterate

[1] Euripides, Ion. 854.

these varieties of tone, but how to compose them into an ordered harmony.

In a modern state, on the other hand, though class distinctions are clearly enough marked, yet the point of view from which they are regarded is fundamentally different. They are attributed rather to accidents of fortune than varieties of nature. The artisan, for example, ranks no doubt lower than the professional man; but no one maintains that he is a different kind of being, incapable by nature, as Aristotle asserts, of the characteristic excellence of man. The distinction admitted is rather one of wealth than of natural calling, and may be obliterated by ability and good luck. Neither in theory nor in practice does the modern state recognize any such gulf as that which, in ancient Greece, separated the freeman from the slave, or the citizen from the non-citizen.

§ 5. THE GREEK STATE PRIMARILY MILITARY, NOT INDUSTRIAL

The source of this divergence of view must be sought in the whole circumstances and character of the Greek states. Founded in the beginning by conquest, many of them still retained, in their internal structure, the marks of their violent origin. The citizens, for example, of Sparta and of Crete, were practically military garrisons, settled in the midst of a hostile population. These were extreme cases; and elsewhere, no doubt, the distinction between the conquerors and the conquered had disappeared. Still, it had sufficed to mould the conception and ideal of the citizen as a member of a privileged and superior class, whose whole energies were devoted to maintaining, by council and war, not only the prosperity, but the very existence of the state. The original citizen, moreover, would be an owner of land, which would be tilled for him by a subject class. Productive labour would be stamped, from the outset, with the stigma of inferiority; commerce would grow up, if at all, outside the limits of the landed aristocracy, and would have a struggle to win for itself any degree of social and political recognition. Such were the conditions that produced the Greek conception of the citizen. In some states, such as Sparta, they continued practically unchanged throughout the best period of Greek history; in others, such as Athens, they were modified by the growth of a commercial population, and where that was the case the conception of the citizen was modified too, and the whole polity assumed a democratic character. Yet never, as we have seen, even in the most democratic states, was the modern conception of equality admitted. For, in the first place, the institution of slavery persisted, to stamp the mass of producers as an inferior caste; and in the second place, trade, even in the states where it was most developed, hardly attained a preponderating influence. The ancient state was and remained primarily military. The great industrial questions which agitate modern states either did not exist at all in Greece, or assumed so simple a form that they did

not rise to the surface of political life.[1]   How curious it is, for example, from the modern point of
view, to find Plato, a citizen of the most important
trading centre of Greece, dismissing in the following
brief sentence the whole commercial legislation of
his ideal state:

"As to those common business transactions between private individuals in the market, including,
if you please, the contracts of artisans, libels, as-
saults, law-proceedings, and the impanelling of ju-
ries, or again questions relating to tariffs, and the
collection of such customs as may be necessary in
the market or in the harbours, and generally all
regulations of the market, the police, the custom-
house, and the like; shall we condescend to legislate
at all on such matters?

"No, it is not worth while to give directions on
these points to good and cultivated men: for in most
cases they will have little difficulty in discovering
all the legislation required." [2]

In fact, throughout his treatise it is the non-
commercial or military class with which Plato is almost exclusively concerned; and in taking that line
he is so far at least in touch with reality that that
class was the one which did in fact predominate in
the Greek state; and that even where, as in Athens,

---

[1] There was, of course, the general opposition between
rich and poor (see below).   But not those infinitely complex relations which are the problems of modern states-
manship.

[2] Plato, Rep. IV. 425.—Translated by Davies and
Vaughan.

the productive class became an important factor in political life, it was never able altogether to overthrow the aristocratic conception of the citizen.

And with that conception, we must add, was bound up the whole Greek view of individual excellence. The inferiority of the artisan and the trader, historically established in the manner we have indicated, was further emphasized by the fact that they were excluded by their calling from the cultivation of the higher personal qualities—from the training of the body by gymnastics and of the mind by philosophy; from habitual conversance with public affairs; from that perfect balance, in a word, of the physical, intellectual, and moral powers, which was only to be attained by a process of self-culture, incompatible with the pursuance of a trade for bread. Such, at any rate, was the opinion of the Greeks. We shall have occasion to return to it later. Meantime, let us sum up the course of our investigation up to the present point.

We have seen that the state, in the Greek view, must be so limited, both in territory and population, that all its citizens might be able to participate in person in its government and defence; that it was based on fundamental class distinctions separating sharply the citizen from the non-citizen, and the slave from the free; that its end and purpose was that all-absorbing corporate activity in which the citizen found the highest expression of himself; and that to that end the inferior classes were regarded as mere means—a point of view which finds its completest expression in the institution of slavery.

§ 6. Forms of Government in the Greek State

While, however, this was the general idea of the Greek state, it would be a mistake to suppose that it was everywhere embodied in a single permanent form of polity. On the contrary, the majority of the states in Greece were in a constant state of flux; revolution succeeded revolution with startling rapidity; and in place of a single fixed type what we really get is a constant transition from one variety to another. The general account we have given ought therefore to be regarded only as a kind of limiting formula, embracing within its range a number of polities distinct and even opposed in character. Of these polities Aristotle, whose work is based on an examination of all the existing states of Greece, recognizes three main varieties: government by the one, government by the few, and government by the many; and each of these is subdivided into two forms, one good, where the government has regard to the well-being of the whole, the other bad, where it has regard only to the well-being of those who govern. The result is six forms, of which three are good, monarchy, aristocracy, and what he calls a "polity" par excellence; three bad, tyranny, oligarchy, and democracy. Of all these forms we have examples in Greek history, and indeed can roughly trace a tendency of the state to evolve through the series of them. But by far the most important, in the historical period, are the two forms known as

Oligarchy and Democracy; and the reason of their importance is that they corresponded roughly to government by the rich and government by the poor. "Rich and poor," says Aristotle, "are the really antagonistic members of a state.   The result is that the character of all existing polities is determined by the predominance of one or other of these classes, and it is the common opinion that there are two polities and two only, *viz.*, Democracy and Oligarchy." [1] In other words, the social distinction between rich and poor was exaggerated in Greece into political antagonism.   In every state there was an oligarchic and a democratic faction; and so fierce was the opposition between them, that we may almost say that every Greek city was in a chronic state of civil war, having become, as Plato puts it, not one city but two, "one comprising the rich and the other the poor, who reside together on the same ground, and are always plotting against one another." [2]

§ 7. FACTION AND ANARCHY

This internal schism which ran through almost every state, came to a head in the great Peloponnesian War which divided Greece at the close of the fifth century, and in which Athens and Sparta, the two chief combatants, represented respectively the democratic and the oligarchic principles.   Each ap-

[1] Arist. Pol. VI. (IV) 1291 b 8.—Translation by Welldon.

[2] Plat. Rep. VIII. §51.—Translation by Davies and Vaughan.

pealed to the kindred faction in the states that were
opposed to them; and every city was divided against
itself, the party that was "out" for the moment plotting with the foreign foe to overthrow the party
that was "in." Thus the general Greek conception
of the ordered state was so far from being realized
that probably at no time in the history of the civi-
lized world has anarchy more complete and cynical
prevailed.

To appreciate the gulf that existed between the
ideal and the fact, we have only to contrast such a
scheme as that set forth in the "Republic" of Plato
with the following description by Thucydides of the
state of Greece during the Peloponnesian War:

"Not long afterwards the whole Hellenic world
was in commotion; in every city the chiefs of the
democracy and of the oligarchy were struggling, the
one to bring in the Athenians, the other the Lacedæmonians. Now in time of peace, men would have
had no excuse for introducing either, and no desire
to do so; but when they were at war and both sides
could easily obtain allies to the hurt of their enemies
and the advantage of themselves, the dissatisfied
party were only too ready to invoke foreign aid.
And revolution brought upon the cities of Hellas
many terrible calamities, such as have been and always will be while human nature remains the same,
but which are more or less aggravated and differ in
character with every new combination of circumstances. In peace and prosperity both states and
individuals are actuated by higher motives, because
they do not fall under the dominion of imperious

necessities; but the war which takes away the comfortable provision of daily life is a hard master, and tends to assimilate men's characters to their conditions.

"When troubles had once begun in the cities, those who followed carried the revolutionary spirit farther and farther, and determined to outdo the report of all who had preceded them by the ingenuity of their enterprises and the atrocity of their revenges. The meaning of words had no longer the same relation to things, but was changed by them as they thought proper. Reckless daring was held to be loyal courage; prudent delay was the excuse of a coward; moderation was the disguise of unmanly weakness; to know everything was to do nothing. Frantic energy was the true quality of a man. A conspirator who wanted to be safe was a recreant in disguise. The lover of violence was always trusted, and his opponent suspected. He who succeeded in a plot was deemed knowing, but a still greater master in craft was he who detected one. On the other hand, he who plotted from the first to have nothing to do with plots was a breaker-up of parties and a poltroon who was afraid of the enemy. In a word, he who could outstrip another in a bad action was applauded, and so was he who encouraged to evil one who had no idea of it. The tie of party was stronger than the tie of blood, because a partisan was more ready to dare without asking why (for party associations are not based upon any established law, nor do they seek the public good; they are formed in defiance of the laws and from self-interest)   The seal of good faith was not divine law, but fellowship in crime. If an enemy when he was in the ascendant offered fair words, the opposite party received them, not in a generous spirit, but by a jealous watchfulness of his actions. Revenge was dearer than self-preservation. Any agreements sworn to by either party, when they could do nothing else, were binding as long as both were powerless. But he who on a favourable opportunity first took courage and struck at his enemy when he saw him off his guard, had greater pleasure in a perfidious than he would have had in an open act of revenge; he congratulated himself that he had taken the safer course, and also that he had overreached his enemy and gained the prize of superior ability. In general the dishonest more easily gain credit for cleverness than the simple for goodness; men take a pride in the one, but are ashamed of the other.

"The cause of all these evils was the love of power originating in avarice and ambition, and the party-spirit which is engendered by them when men are fairly embarked in a contest. For the leaders on either side used specious names, the one party professing to uphold the constitutional equality of the many, the other the wisdom of an aristocracy, while they made the public interests, to which in name they were devoted, in reality their prize. Striving in every way to overcome each other, they committed the most monstrous crimes; yet even these were surpassed by the magnitude of their revenges which they pursued to the very utmost, neither party observing any definite limits either of justice or public expediency, but both alike making the caprice of the moment their law. Either by the help of an unrighteous sentence, or grasping power with the strong hand, they were eager to satiate the impatience of party spirit. Neither faction cared for religion; but any fair pretense which succeeded in effecting some odious purpose was greatly lauded. And the citizens who were of neither party fell a prey to both; either they were disliked because they held aloof, or men were jealous of their surviving.

"Thus revolution gave birth to every form of wickedness in Hellas. The simplicity which is so large an element in a noble nature was laughed to scorn and disappeared. An attitude of perfidious antagonism everywhere prevailed; for there was no word binding enough, nor oath terrible enough to reconcile enemies. Each man was strong only in the conviction that nothing was secure; he must look to his own safety, and could not afford to trust others. Inferior intellects generally succeeded best. For aware of their own deficiencies, and fearing the capacities of their opponents, for whom they were no match in powers of speech, and whose subtle wits were likely to anticipate them in contriving evil, they struck boldly and at once. But the cleverer sort, presuming in their arrogance that they would be aware in time, and disdaining to act when they could think, were taken off their guard and easily destroyed." [1]

The general indictment thus drawn up by

[1] Thuc. III. 82.—Translated by Jowett.

Thucydides is amply illustrated by the events of war which he describes. On one occasion, for example, the Athenians were blockading Mitylene; the government, an oligarchy, was driven to arm the people for the defence; the people, having obtained arms, immediately demanded political rights, under threat of surrendering the city to the foreign foe; and the government, rather than concede their claims, surrendered it themselves. Again, Megara, we learn, was twice betrayed, once by the democrats to the Athenians, and again by the oligarchs to the Lacedæmonians. At Leontini the Syracusans were called in to drive out the popular party. And at Corcyra the people, having got the better of their aristocratic opponents, proceeded to a general massacre which extended over seven days, with every variety of moral and physical atrocity.

Such is the view of the political condition of Greece given to us by a contemporary observer towards the close of the fifth century, and it is a curious comment on the Greek idea of the state. That idea, as we saw, was an ordered inequality, political as well as social; and in certain states, and notably in Sparta, it was successfully embodied in a stable form. But in the majority of the Greek states it never attained to more than a fluctuating and temporary realization. The inherent contradiction was too extreme for the attempted reconciliation; the inequalities refused to blend in a harmony of divergent tones, but asserted themselves in the dissonance of civil war.

§ 8. PROPERTY AND THE COMMUNISTIC IDEAL

And, as we have seen, this internal schism of the Greek state was as much social as political. The "many" and the "few" were identified respectively with the poor and the rich; and the struggle was thus at bottom as much economic as political. Government by an oligarchy was understood to mean the exploitation of the masses by the classes. "An oligarchy," says a democrat, as reported by Thucydides, "while giving the people the full share of danger, not merely takes too much of the good things, but absolutely monopolizes them." [1] And, similarly, the advent of democracy was held to imply the spoliation of the classes in the interest of the masses, either by excessive taxation, by an abuse of the judicial power to fine, or by any other of the semi-legal devices of oppression which the majority in power have always at their command. This substantial identity of rich and poor, respectively, with oligarch and democrat may be further illustrated by the following passage from Aristotle:

"In consequence of the political disturbances and contentions between the commons on the one hand and the rich on the other, whichever party happens to get the better of its opponents, instead of establishing a polity of a broad and equal kind, assumes political supremacy as a prize of the victory, and sets up either a Democracy or an Oligarchy." [2]

---

[1] Thuc. VI. 32.—Translated by Jowett.
[2] Arist. Pol. VI. (IV) 1296 a 27.—Translation by Welldon.

We see, then, that it was the underlying question of property that infused so strong a rancour into the party struggles of Greece. From the very earliest period, in fact, we find it to have been the case that political revolution was prompted by economic causes. Debt was the main factor of the crisis which led to the legislation of Solon; and a re-division of the land was one of the measures attributed to Lycurgus.[1] As population increased, and, in the maritime states, commerce and trade developed, the problem of poverty became increasingly acute; and though it was partially met by the emigration of the surplus population to colonies, yet in the fifth and fourth centuries we find it prominent and pressing both in practical politics and in speculation. Nothing can illustrate better how familiar the topic was, and to what free theorizing it had led, than the passages in which it is treated in the comedies of Aristophanes. Here, for example, is an extract from the "Ecclesiazusæ" which it may be worth while to insert as a contribution to an argument that belongs to every age.

PRAXAGORA. I tell you that we are all to share alike and have everything in common, instead of one being rich and another poor, and one having hundreds of acres and another not enough to make him a grave, and one a houseful

[1] I have not thought it necessary for my purpose, here or elsewhere, to discuss the authenticity of the statements made by Greek authors about Lycurgus.

of servants and another not even a paltry foot-boy. I am going to introduce communism and universal equality.

BLEPSYRUS. How communism?

PRAX. That's just what I was going to tell you. First of all, everybody's money and land and anything else he may possess will be made common property. Then we shall maintain you all out of the common stock, with due regard to economy and thrift.

BLEPS. But how about those who have no land, but only money that they can hide?

PRAX. It will all go to the public purse. To keep anything back will be perjury.

BLEPS. Perjury! Well, if you come to that, it was by perjury it was all acquired.

PRAX. And then, money won't be the least use to anyone.

BLEPS. Why not?

PRAX. Because nobody will be poor. Everybody will have everything he wants, bread, salt-fish, barley-cake, clothes, wine, garlands, chickpeas. So what will be the good of keeping anything back? Answer that if you can!

BLEPS. Isn't it just the people who have all these things that are the greatest thieves?

PRAX. No doubt, under the old laws. But now, when everything will be in common, what will be the good of keeping anything back?

BLEPS. Who will do the field work?

PRAX. The slaves; all you will have to do is to

dress and go out to dinner in the evening.

BLEPS. But what about the clothes? How are they to be provided?

PRAX. What you have now will do to begin with, and afterwards we shall make them for you ourselves.

BLEPS. Just one thing more! Supposing a man were to lose his suit in the courts, where are the damages to come from? It would not be fair to take the public funds.

PRAX. But there won't be any lawsuits at all!

BLEPS. That will mean ruin to a good many people.

BYSTANDER. Just my idea!

PRAX. Why should there be any?

BLEPS. Why! for reasons enough, heaven knows! For instance, a man might repudiate his debts.

PRAX. In that case, where did the man who lent the money get it from? Clearly, since everything is in common, he must have stolen it!

BLEPS. So he must! An excellent idea! But now tell me this. When fellows come to blows over their cups, where are the damages to come from?

PRAX. From the rations! A man won't be in such a hurry to make a row when his belly has to pay for it.

BLEPS. One thing more! Will there be no more thieves?

PRAX. Why should anyone steal what is his own?

BLEPS. And won't one be robbed of one's cloak at night?

PRAX. Not if you sleep at home!

BLEPS. Nor yet, if one sleeps out, as one used to do?

PRAX. No, for there will be enough and to spare for all. And even if a thief does try to strip a man, he will give up his cloak of his own accord. What would be the good of fighting? He has only to go and get another, and a better, from the public stores.

BLEPS. And will there be no more gambling?

PRAX. What will there be to play for?

BLEPS. And how about house accommodation?

PRAX. That will be the same for all. I tell you I am going to turn the whole city into one huge house, and break down all the partitions, so that everyone may have free access to everyone else.[1]

The "social problem," then, had clearly arisen in ancient Greece, though no doubt in an infinitely simpler form than that in which it is presented to ourselves; and it might perhaps have been expected that the Greeks, with their notion of the supremacy of the state, would have adopted some drastic public measure to meet it. And, in fact, in the earlier period of their history, as has been indicated above, we do find sweeping revolutions effected in the distribution of property. In Athens, Solon cancelled debt secured on person or property; and in Sparta Lycurgus is said to have resumed the whole of the land for the state, and redivided it equally among the

[1] Aristoph. Eccles. 590.

citizens. We have also traces of laws existing in other states to regulate in the interests of equality the possession and transfer of land. But it does not appear that any attempt was made in any state permanently to control by public authority the production and distribution of wealth.

Meantime, however, the problem of social inequality was exercising the minds of political theorists; and we have notice of various schemes for an ideal polity framed upon communistic principles. Of these the most important, and the only one preserved to us, is the celebrated "Republic" of Plato; and never, it may be safely asserted, was a plan of society framed so consistent, harmonious and beautiful in itself, or so indifferent to the actual capacities of mankind. Following out what we have already indicated as the natural drift of Greek ideas, the philosopher separates off on the one hand the productive class, who are to have no political rights; and on the other the class of soldiers and governors. It is the latter alone with whom he seriously concerns himself; and the scheme he draws up for them is uncompromisingly communistic. After being purged, by an elaborate education, of all the egoistic passions, they are to live together, having all things in common, devoted heart and soul to the public good, and guiltless even of a desire for any private possession or advantage of their own. "In the first place, no one," says Plato, " should possess any private property, if it can possibly be avoided; secondly, no one should have a dwelling or storehouse into which all who please may not enter; whatever necessaries are required by temperate and courageous men, who are trained to war, they should receive by regular appointment from their fellow-citizens, as wages for their services, and the amount should be such as to leave neither a surplus on the year's consumption nor a deficit; and they should attend common messes and live together as men do in a camp: as for gold and silver, we must tell them that they are in perpetual possession of a divine species of the precious metals placed in their souls by the gods themselves, and therefore have no need of the earthly one; that in fact it would be profanation to pollute their spiritual riches by mixing them with the possession of mortal gold, because the world's coinage has been the cause of countless impieties, whereas theirs is undefiled: therefore to them, as distinguished from the rest of the people, it is forbidden to handle or touch gold and silver, or enter under the same roof with them, or to wear them in their dresses, or to drink out of the precious metals. If they follow these rules, they will be safe themselves and the saviours of the city; but whenever they come to possess lands, and houses, and money of their own, they will be householders and cultivators instead of guardians, and will become hostile masters of their fellow-citizens rather than their allies; and so they will spend their whole lives, hating and hated, plotting and plotted against, standing in more frequent and intense alarm of their enemies at home than of their enemies abroad; by which time they and the rest of the city will be running on the very brink of ruin." [1]

The passage is interesting, if only as an illustration of the way in which Plato had been impressed by the evil results of the institution of private property. But as a contribution to political theory it was open to severe attack from the representatives of experience and common sense. Of these, the chief was Aristotle, whose criticism has been preserved to us, and who, while admitting that Plato's scheme has a plausible appearance of philanthropy, maintains that it is inapplicable to the facts of human nature. To this conclusion, indeed, even Plato himself was driven in the end; for in his later work, the "Laws," although he still asserts that community of goods would be the ideal institution, he reluctantly abandons it as a basis for a possible state. On the other hand, he endeavours by the most stringent regulations, to prevent the growth of inequalities of wealth. He distributes the land in equal lots among his citizens, prohibiting either purchase or subdivision; limits the possession of money to the amount required for daily exchange; and forbids lending on interest. The object of a legislator, he declares, is to make not a great but a happy city. But only the good are happy, and goodness and wealth are incompatible. The legislator, therefore, will not allow his citizens to be wealthy, any more than he will allow them to be poor. He will seek to establish by law the happy mean; and to this

[1] Plato, Rep. III. 416.—Translation by Davies and Vaughan.

end, if he despair of the possibility of a thorough-
going communism, will legislate at least as indicated
above.

The uncompromising idealism of Plato's scheme,
with its assumption of the indefinite plasticity of
human nature, is of course peculiar to himself, not
typical of Greek ideas. But it is noticeable that
Aristotle, who is a far better representative of the
average Greek mind, exhibits the same mistrust of
the accumulation of private property. In the beginning of his "Politics" he distinguishes two kinds
of money-making, one natural, that which is pursued for the sake of a livelihood, the other unnatural,
that which is pursued for the sake of accumulation.
"The motive of this latter," he says, "is a desire
for life instead of for good life"; and its most hateful method is that of usury, the unnatural breeding
of money out of money. And though he rejects as
impracticable the compulsory communism of Plato's
"Republic," yet he urges as the ideal solution that
property, while owned by individuals, should be held
as in trust for the common good; and puts before the legislator the problem: "so to dispose the
higher natures that they are unwilling, and the
lower that they are unable to aggrandize themselves." [1]

Such views as these, it may be noted, interesting
though they be, as illustrating how keenly the thinkers of ancient Greece had realized the drawbacks
of private property, have but the slightest bearing

[1] Aristotle, Pol. II. 7. 1267 b 6.—Translation by
Welldon.

on the conditions of our own time. The complexity
and extent of modern industry have given rise to
quite new problems, and quite new schemes for their
solution; and especially have forced into prominence
the point of view of the producers themselves. To
Greek thinkers it was natural to approach the question of property from the side of the governing class
or of the state as a whole. The communism of
Plato, for example, applied only to the "guardians"
and soldiers, and not to the productive class on
whom they depended; and so completely was he
pre-occupied with the former to the exclusion of the
latter, that he dismisses in a single sentence, as unworthy the legislator's detailed attention, the whole
apparatus of labour and exchange. To regard the
"working-class" as the most important section of the
community, to substitute for the moral or political
the economic standpoint, and to conceive society
merely as a machine for the production and distribution of wealth, would have been impossible to an
ancient Greek. Partly by the simplicity of the economic side of the society with which he was acquainted, partly by the habit of regarding the la-
bouring class as a mere means to the maintenance
of the rest, he was led, even when he had to deal
with the problem of poverty and wealth, to regard
it rather from the point of view of the stability
and efficiency of the state, than from that of the
welfare of the producers themselves. The modern
attitude is radically different; a revolution has been
effected both in the conditions of industry and in the
way in which they are regarded; and the practice and

the speculation of the Greek city-states have for us
an interest which, great as it is, is philosophic rather
than practical.

§ 9. Sparta

The preceding attempt at a general sketch of the
nature of the Greek state is inevitably loose and
misleading to this extent, that it endeavours to comprehend in a single view polities of the most varied
and discrepant character. To remedy, as far as
may be, this defect, to give an impression, more definite and more complete, of the variety and scope
of the political experience of the Greeks, let us
examine a little more in detail the character of the
two states which were at once the most prominent
and the most opposed in their achievement and their
aim—the state of Sparta on the one hand, and that
of Athens on the other. It was these two cities that
divided the hegemony of Greece; they represent the
extremes of the two forms—oligarchy and democracy—under which, as we saw, the Greek polities
fall; and from a sufficient acquaintance with them
we may gather a fairly complete idea of the whole
range of Greek political life.

In Sparta we see one extreme of the political
development of Greece, and the one which approaches nearest, perhaps, to the characteristic
Greek type. Of that type, it is true, it was an exaggeration, and was recognized as such by the best
thinkers of Greece; but just for that reason it is
the more interesting and instructive as an exhibi-

tion of a distinctive aspect of Greek civilization.

The Spartan state was composed of a small body of citizens—the Spartiatae or Spartans proper—encamped in the midst of a hostile population to whom they allowed no political rights and by whose labour they were supplied with the necessaries of life. The distinction between the citizen class on the one hand and the productive class on the other was thus as clearly and sharply drawn as possible. It was even exaggerated; for the citizens were a band of conquerors, the productive class a subject race, perpetually on the verge of insurrection, and only kept in restraint by such measures as secret assassination. The result was to draw together the small band of Spartiatae into a discipline so rigorous and close that under it everything was sacrificed to the necessity of self-preservation; and the bare maintenance of the state became the end for which every individual was born, and lived, and died. This discipline, according to tradition, had been devised by a single legislator, Lycurgus, and it was maintained intact for several centuries. Its main features may be summarized as follows:

The production and rearing of children, to begin at the beginning, instead of being left to the caprice of individuals, was controlled and regulated by the state. The women, in the first place, were trained by physical exercise for the healthy performance of the duties of motherhood; they were taught to run and wrestle naked, like the youths, to dance and sing in public, and to associate freely with men. Marriage was permitted only in the prime of life;

and a free intercourse, outside its limits, between healthy men and women, was encouraged and approved by public opinion. Men who did not marry were subject to social and civic disabilities. The children, as soon as they were born, were submitted to the inspection of the elders of their tribe; if strong and well formed, they were reared; if not, they were allowed to die.

A healthy stock having been thus provided as a basis, every attention was devoted to its appropriate training. The infants were encouraged from the beginning in the free use of their limbs, unhampered by swaddling-clothes, and were accustomed to endure without fear darkness and solitude, and to cure themselves of peevishness and crying. At the age of seven the boys were taken away from the charge of their parents, and put under the superintendence of a public official. Their education, on the intellectual side, was slight enough, comprising only such rudiments as reading and writing; but on the moral side it was stringent and severe. Gathered into groups under the direction of elder youths—"monitors" we might call them—they were trained to a discipline of iron endurance. One garment served them for the whole year; they went without shoes, and slept on beds of rushes plucked with their own hands. Their food was simple, and often enough they had to go without it. Every moment of the day they were under inspection and supervision, for it was the privilege and the duty of every citizen to admonish and punish not only his own but other people's children. At supper they waited at table on their elders, answered their questions and endured their jests. In the streets they were taught to walk in silence, their hands folded in their cloaks, their eyes cast down, their heads never turning to right or left. Their gymnastic and military training was incessant; wherever they met, we are told, they be-gan to box; under the condition, however, that they were bound to separate at the command of any by-stander. To accustom them early to the hardships of a campaign, they were taught to steal their food from the mess-tables of their elders; if they were detected they were beaten for their clumsiness, and went without their dinner. Nothing was omitted, on the moral or physical side, to make them efficient members of a military state. Nor was the disci-pline relaxed when they reached years of maturity. For, in fact, the whole city was a camp. Family life was obliterated by public activity. The men dined together in messes, rich and poor alike, shar-ing the same coarse and simple food. Servants, dogs, and horses, were regarded as common prop-erty. Luxury was strictly forbidden. The only currency in circulation was of iron, so cumbrous that it was impossible to accumulate or conceal it. The houses were as simple as possible, the roofs shaped only with the axe, and the doors with the saw; the furniture and fittings corresponded, plain but per-fectly made. The nature of the currency practically prohibited commerce, and no citizen was allowed to be engaged in any mechanical trade. Agriculture was the main industry, and every Spartan had, or was supposed to have, a landed estate, cultivated by serfs who paid him a yearly rent. In complete accordance with the Greek ideal, it was a society of soldier-citizens, supported by an inferior productive class.

In illustration of this point the following curious anecdote may be quoted from Plutarch. During one of the wars in which Sparta and her allies were engaged, the allies complained that they, who were the majority of the army, had been forced into a quarrel which concerned nobody but the Spartans. Whereupon Agesilaus, the Spartan king, "devised this expedient to show the allies were not the greater number. He gave orders that all the allies, of whatever country, should sit down promiscuously on one side, and all the Lacedæmonians on the other: which being done, he commanded a herald to proclaim, that all the potters of both divisions should stand out; then all the blacksmiths; then all the masons; next the carpenters; and so he went through all the handicrafts. By this time almost all the allies were risen, but of the Lacedæmonians not a man, they being by law forbidden to learn any mechanical business; and now Agesilaus laughed and said, "You see, my friends, how many more, soldiers we send out than you do." [1]

And certainly, so far as its immediate ends were concerned, this society of soldier-citizens was singularly successful. The courage and efficiency of Spartan troops were notorious, and were maintained indeed not only by the training we have described, but by social penalties attached to cowardice. A

[1] Plut. Agesilaus.—Translation by Clough.

man who had disgraced himself in battle was a pariah in his native land. No one would eat with him, no one would wrestle with him; in the dance he must take the lowest place; he must give the wall at meetings in the street, and resign his seat even to younger men; he must dress and bear himself humbly, under penalty of blows, and suffer the reproaches of women and of boys. Death plainly would be preferable to such a life; and we are not surprised to hear that the discipline and valour of Spartan troops was celebrated far and wide. Here is a description of them, given by one of themselves to the Persian king when he was projecting the invasion of Greece:

"Brave are all the Greeks who dwell in any Dorian land; but what I am about to say does not concern all, but only the Lacedæmonians. First, then, come what may, they will never accept thy terms, which would reduce Greece to slavery; and further, they are sure to join battle with thee, though all the rest of Greece should submit to thy will. As for their numbers, do not ask how many they are, that their resistance should be a possible thing; for if a thousand of them should take the field, they will meet thee in battle, and so will any number, be it less than this, or be it more.

"When they fight singly, they are as good men as any in the world, and when they fight in a body, they are the bravest of all. For though they be freemen, they are not in all respects free; Law is the master whom they own; and this master they fear more than thy subjects fear thee. Whatever he com-

mands they do; and his commandment is always the
same: it forbids them to flee in battle, whatever the
number of their foes, and requires them to stand
firm, and either to conquer or die." [1]

The practical illustration of this speech is the battle of Thermopylae, where 300 Spartans kept at bay
the whole Persian host, till they were betrayed from
the rear and killed fighting to a man.

The Spartan state, then, justified itself according
to its own ideal; but how limited that ideal was will
be clear from our sketch. The individual, if it cannot be said that he was sacrificed to the state—for
he recognized the life of the state as his own—was
at any rate starved upon one side of his nature as
much as he was hypertrophied upon the other.
Courage, obedience, and endurance were developed
in excess; but the free play of passion and thought,
the graces and arts of life, all that springs from the
spontaneity of nature, were crushed out of existence
under this stern and rigid rule. "None of them,"
says Plutarch, an enthusiastic admirer of the Spartan polity, "none of them was left alone to live as
he chose; but passing their time in the city as though
it were a camp, their manner of life and their avocations ordered with a view to the public good, they
regarded themselves as belonging, not to themselves,
but to their country." [2]   And Plato, whose ideal republic was based so largely upon the Spartan model,
has marked nevertheless as the essential defect of

[1] Herodotus VII. 102, 4.—Translation by Rawlinson.
[2] Plut. Lycurgus, ch. 24.

their polity its insistence on military virtue to the exclusion of everything else, and its excessive accentuation of the corporate aspect of life. "Your military way of life," he says, "is modelled after the camp, and is not like that of dwellers in cities; and you have your young men herding and feeding together like young colts. No one takes his own individual colt and drags him away from his fellows against his will, raging and foaming, and gives him a groom for him alone, and trains and rubs him down privately, and gives him the qualities in education which will make him not only a good soldier, but also a governor of a state and of cities. Such a one would be a greater warrior than he of whom Tyrtæus sings; and he would honour courage everywhere, but always as the fourth, and not as the first part of virtue, either in individuals or state." [1]

The Spartan state, in fact, by virtue of that excellence which was also its defect—the specializing of the individual on the side of discipline and rule—carried within it the seeds of its own destruction. The tendencies which Lycurgus had endeavoured to repress by external regulation reasserted themselves in his despite. He had intended once for all both to limit and to equalize private property; but already as early as the fifth century Spartans had accumulated gold which they deposited in temples in foreign states; the land fell, by inheritance and gift, into the hands of a small minority; the number of the citizens was reduced, not only by war, but by

[1] Plato, Laws. II. 666 e.—Translation by Jowett.

the disfranchisement attending inability to contribute to the common mess-tables; till at last we find no more than 700 Spartan families, and of these no more than 100 possessing estates in land.

And this decline from within was hastened by external events. The constitution devised for a small state encamped amidst a hostile population, broke down under the weight of imperial power. The conquest of Athens by Sparta was the signal of her own collapse. The power and wealth she had won at a stroke alienated her sons from her discipline. Generals and statesmen who had governed like kings the wealthy cities of the east were unable to adapt themselves again to the stern and narrow rules of Lycurgus. They rushed into freedom and enjoyment, into the unfettered use of their powers, with an energy proportional to their previous restraint. The features of the human face broke through the fair but lifeless mask of ancient law; and the Spartan, ceasing to be a Spartan, both rose and fell to the level of a man.

§ 10. Athens

In the institutions of Sparta we see, carried to its farthest point, one side of the complex Greek nature—their capacity for discipline and law. Athens, the home of a different stock, gives us the other extreme—their capacity for rich and spontaneous individual development. To pass from Sparta to Athens, is to pass from a barracks to a playing-field. All the beauty, all the grace, all the joy of Greece; all that chains the desire of mankind,

with a yearning that is never stilled, to that one
golden moment in the past, whose fair and balanced
interplay of perfect flesh and soul no later gains of
thought can compensate, centres about that bright
and stately city of romance, the home of Pericles
and all the arts, whence from generation to generation has streamed upon ages less illustrious an influence at once the sanest and the most inspired of all
that have shaped the secular history of the world.
Girt by mountain and sea, by haunted fountain and
sacred grove, shaped and adorned by the master
hands of Pheidias and Polygnotus and filled with
the breath of passion and song by Euripides and
Plato, Athens, famed alike for the legended deeds of
heroes and gods and for the feats of her human sons
in council, art, and war, is a name, to those who have
felt her spell, more familiar and more dear than any
of the few that mark with gold the sombre scroll of
history.   And still across the years we feel the throb
of the glorious verse that broke in praise of his native land from the lips of Euripides:

"Happy of yore were the children of race divine,
Happy the sons of old Erechtheus' line
        Who in their holy state
        With hands inviolate
Gather the flower of wisdom far-renowned,
Lightly lifting their feet in the lucid air
Where the sacred nine, the Pierid Muses, bare
        Harmonia golden-crowned.

There in the wave from fair Kephisus flowing
Kupris sweetens the winds and sets them blowing

> Over the delicate land;
> And ever with joyous hand
> Braiding her fragrant hair with the blossom of roses,
> She sendeth the Love that dwelleth in Wisdom's place
> That every virtue may quicken and every grace
> In the hearts where she reposes." [1]

And this, the Athens of poetry and art, is but another aspect of the Athens of political history. The same individuality, the same free and passionate energy that worked in the hearts of her sculptors and her poets, moulded also and inspired her city life. In contradistinction to the stern and rigid discipline of Sparta, the Athenian citizen displayed the resource, the versatility and the zeal that only freedom and self-reliance can teach. The contrast is patent at every stage of the history of the two states, and has been acutely set forth by Thucydides in the speech which he puts into the mouths of the Corinthian allies of Sparta:

"You have never considered," they say to the Lacedæmonians, "what manner of men are these Athenians with whom you will have to fight, and how utterly unlike yourselves. They are revolutionary, equally quick in the conception and in the execution of every new plan; while you are conservative—careful only to keep what you have, originating nothing, and not acting even when action is most necessary. They are bold beyond their strength; they run risks which prudence would condemn; and in the midst of misfortunes they are full of hope. Whereas it is

[1] Eurip. Medea, 825.

your nature, though strong, to act feebly; when your
plans are most prudent, to distrust them; and when
calamities come upon you, to think that you will
never be delivered from them.   They are impetuous,
and you are dilatory; they are always abroad, and
you are always at home.   For they hope to gain
something by leaving their homes; but you are
afraid that any new enterprise may imperil what
you have already.   When conquerors, they pursue
their victory to the utmost; when defeated, they fall
back the least.   Their bodies they devote to their
country as though they belonged to other men; their
true self is their mind, which is most truly their own
when employed in her service.   When they do not
carry out an intention which they have formed, they
seem to have sustained a personal bereavement;
when an enterprise succeeds, they have gained a
mere instalment of what is to come; but if they fail,
they at once conceive new hopes and so fill up the
void.   With them alone to hope is to have, for they
lose not a moment in the execution of an idea.   This
is the life-long task, full of danger and toil, which
they are always imposing upon themselves.   None
enjoy their good things less, because they are always
seeking for more.   To do their duty is their only
holiday, and they deem the quiet of inaction to be as
disagreeable as the most tiresome business.   If a
man should say of them, in a word, that they were
born neither to have peace themselves nor to allow
peace to other men, he would simply speak the
truth." [1]

[1] Thuc. I. 70.—Translated by Jowett.

The qualities here set forth by Thucydides as
characteristic of the Athenians, were partly the
cause and partly the effect of their political constitution. The history of Athens, indeed, is the very
antithesis to that of Sparta. In place of a type fixed
at a stroke and enduring for centuries, she presents
a series of transitions through the whole range of
polities, to end at last in a democracy so extreme
that it refuses to be included within the limits of the
general formula of the Greek state.

Seldom, indeed, has "equality" been pushed to so
extreme a point as it was, politically at least, in
ancient Athens. The class of slaves, it is true, existed there as in every other state; but among the
free citizens, who included persons of every rank, no
political distinction at all was drawn. All of them,
from the lowest to the highest, had the right to speak
and vote in the great assembly of the people which
was the ultimate authority; all were eligible to every
administrative post; all sat in turns as jurors in the
law-courts. The disabilities of poverty were minimized by payment for attendance in the assembly
and the courts. And, what is more extraordinary,
even distinctions of ability were levelled by the practice of filling all offices, except the highest, by lot.

Had the citizens been a class apart, as was the
case in Sparta, had they been subjected from the
cradle to a similar discipline and training, forbidden
to engage in any trade or business, and consecrated
to the service of the state, there would have been
nothing surprising in this uncompromising assertion
of equality. But in Athens the citizenship was ex-

tended to every rank and calling: the poor man
jostled the rich, the shopman the aristocrat, in the
Assembly; cobblers, carpenters, smiths, farmers,
merchants, and retail traders met together with the
ancient landed gentry, to debate and conclude on
national affairs; and it was from such varied elements as these that the lot impartially chose the
officials of the law, the revenue, the police, the high-
ways, the markets, and the ports, as well as the
jurors at whose mercy stood reputation, fortune, and
life. The consequence was that in Athens, at least
in the later period of her history, the middle and
lower classes tended to monopolize political power.
Of the popular leaders, Cleon, the most notorious,
was a tanner; another was a baker, another a cattle-
dealer. Influence belonged to those who had the
gift of leading the mass; and in that competition the
man of tongue, of energy, and of resource, was more
than a match for the aristocrat of birth and intellect.
The constitution of Athens, then, was one of
political equality imposed upon social inequality.
To illustrate the point we may quote a passage from
Aristophanes which shows at once the influence
exercised by the trading class and the disgust with
which that influence was regarded by the aristocracy
whom the poet represents. The passage is taken
from the "Knights," a comedy written to discredit
Cleon, and turning upon the expulsion of the notorious tanner from the good graces of Demos, by
the superior impudence and address of a sausage-
seller. Demosthenes, a general of the aristocratic

party, is communicating to the latter the destiny
that awaits him.

DEMOSTHENES (*to the* SAUSAGE-SELLER *gravely*).
Set these poor wares aside; and now—bow down
To the ground; and adore the powers of earth and
    heaven.
    S.-S. Heigh-day! Why, what do you mean?
DEM.   O happy man!
Unconscious of your glorious destiny,
Now mean and unregarded; but to-morrow,
The mightiest of the mighty, Lord of Athens.
    S.-S. Come, master, what's the use of making game?
Why can't ye let me wash my guts and tripe,
And sell my sausages in peace and quiet?
    DEM. O simple mortal, cast those thoughts aside!
Bid guts and tripe farewell! Look here! Behold!
                   (*pointing to the audience*)
The mighty assembled multitude before ye!
    S.-S. (*with a grumble of indifference*).
I see 'em.
    DEM. You shall be their lord and master,
The sovereign and the ruler of them all,
Of the assemblies and tribunals, fleets and armies;
You shall trample down the Senate under foot,
Confound and crush the generals and commanders,
Arrest, imprison, and confine in irons,
And feast and fornicate in the Council House.
    S.-S. Are there any means of making a great man
Of a sausage-selling fellow such as I?
    DEM. The very means you have, must make ye so,
Low breeding, vulgar birth, and impudence,
These, these must make ye, what you're meant to be.
    S.-S. I can't imagine that I'm good for much.

DEM. Alas! But why do ye say so? What's the
      meaning
Of these misgivings? I discern within ye
A promise and an inward consciousness
Of greatness. Tell me truly: are ye allied
To the families of gentry?
    S.-S.   Naugh, not I;
I'm come from a common ordinary kindred,
Of the lower order.
    DEM.   What a happiness!
What a footing will it give ye! What a groundwork
For confidence and favour at your outset!
    S.-S. But bless ye! only consider my education!
I can but barely read . . . in a kind of way.
    DEM. That makes against ye!—the only thing
      against ye—
The being able to read, in any way:
For now no lead nor influence is allowed
To liberal arts or learned education,
But to the brutal, base, and underbred.
Embrace then and hold fast the promises
Which the oracles of the gods announce to you.[1]

We have here an illustration, one among many
that might be given, of the political equality that
prevailed in Athens. It shows us how completely
that distinction between the military or governing,
and the productive class, which belonged to the
normal Greek conception of the state, had been
broken down, on the side at least of privilege and
right, though not on that of social estimation, in this
most democratic of the ancient states. Politically,
the Athenian trader and the Athenian artisan was

[1] Aristoph. Knights. 155.—Translation by Frere.

the equal of the aristocrat of purest blood; and so far the government of Athens was a genuine democracy.

But so far only. For in Athens, as in every Greek state, the greater part of the population was unfree; and the government, which was a democracy from the point of view of the freeman, was an oligarchy from the point of view of the slave. For the slaves, by the nature of their position, had no political rights; and they were more than half of the population. It is noticeable, however, that the freedom and individuality which was characteristic of the Athenian citizen, appears to have reacted favourably on the position of the slaves. Not only had they, to a certain extent, the protection of the law against the worst excesses of their masters, but they were allowed a license of bearing and costume which would not have been tolerated in any other state. A contemporary writer notes that in dress and general appearance Athenian slaves were not to be distinguished from citizens, that they were permitted perfect freedom of speech; and that it was open to them to acquire a fortune and to live in ease and luxury. In Sparta, he says, the slave stands in fear of the freeman, but in Athens this is not the case; and certainly the bearing of the slaves introduced into the Athenian comedy does not indicate any undue subservience. Slavery at the best is an undemocratic institution; but in Athens it appears to have been made as democratic as its nature would admit.

We find, then, in the Athenian state, the conception of equality pushed to the farthest extreme at all compatible with Greek ideas; pushed, we may fairly say, at last to an undue excess; for the great days of Athens were those when she was still under the influence of her aristocracy, and when the popular zeal evoked by her free institutions was directed by members of the leisured and cultivated class. The most glorious age of Athenian history closes with the death of Pericles; and Pericles was a man of noble family, freely chosen, year after year, by virtue of his personal qualities, to exercise over this democratic nation a dictatorship of character and brain. It is into his mouth that Thucydides has put that great panegyric of Athens, which sets forth to all time the type of an ideal state and the record of what was at least partially achieved in the greatest of the Greek cities:

"Our form of government does not enter into rivalry with the institutions of others. We do not copy our neighbours, but are an example to them. It is true that we are called a democracy, for the administration is in the hands of the many and not of the few. But while the law secures equal justice to all alike in their private disputes, the claim of excellence is also recognized; and when a citizen is in any way distinguished, he is preferred to the public service, not as a matter of privilege, but as the reward of merit. Neither is poverty a bar, but a man may benefit his country whatever be the obscurity of his condition. There is no exclusiveness in our public life, and in our private intercourse we are not suspicious of one another, nor angry with our neighbour if he does what he likes; we do not put on sour looks at him, which, though harmless, are not pleasant. While we are thus unconstrained in our private intercourse, a spirit of reverence pervades our public acts; we are prevented from doing wrong by respect for authority and for the laws, having an especial regard for those which are ordained for the protection of the injured, as well as for those unwritten laws which bring upon the transgressor of them the reprobation of the general sentiment.

"And we have not forgotten to provide for our weary spirits many relaxations from toil; we have regular games and sacrifices throughout the year; at home the style of our life is refined; and the delight which we daily feel in all these things helps to banish melancholy. Because of the greatness of our city the fruits of the whole earth flow in upon us, so that we enjoy the goods of other countries as freely as of our own.

"Then, again, our military training is in many respects superior to that of our adversaries. Our city is thrown open to the world, and we never expel a foreigner or prevent him from seeing or learning anything of which the secret if revealed to an enemy might profit him. We rely not upon management and trickery, but upon our own hearts and hands. And in the matter of education, whereas they from early youth are always undergoing laborious exercises which are to make them brave, we live at ease, and yet are ready to face the perils which they face.

"If, then, we prefer to meet danger with a light

heart but without laborious training, and with a
courage which is gained by habit and not enforced
by law, are we not greatly the gainers?   Since we do
not anticipate the pain, although when the hour
comes, we can be as brave as those who never allow
themselves to rest; and thus too our city is equally
admirable in peace and in war.   For we are lovers
of the beautiful, yet simple in our tastes, and we
cultivate   the   mind   without   loss   of   manliness.
Wealth we employ, not for talk and ostentation, but
when there is a real use for it.   To avow poverty
with us is no disgrace; the true disgrace is in doing
nothing to avoid it.   An Athenian citizen does not
neglect the state because he takes care of his own
household; and even those of us who are engaged
in business have a very fair idea of politics.   We
alone regard a man who takes no interest in public
affairs, not as a harmless, but as a useless character;
and if few of us are originators, we are all sound
judges of a policy.   The great impediment to action
is, in our opinion, not discussion but the want of
that   knowledge   which   is   gained   by   discussion
preparatory to action.   For we have a peculiar
power of thinking before we act, and of acting too,
whereas other men are courageous from ignorance
but hesitate upon reflection.   And they are surely
to be esteemed the bravest spirits who have the clearest sense of the pains and pleasures of life, but do
not on that account shrink from danger.

"To sum up, I say that Athens is the school of
Hellas, and that the individual Athenian in his own
person seems to have the power of adapting himself

to the most varied forms of action with the utmost versatility and grace.   This is no passing and idle word, but truth and fact; and the assertion is verified by the position to which these qualities have raised the state.   For in the hour of trial Athens alone among her contemporaries is superior to the report of her.   No enemy who comes against her is indignant at the reverses which he sustains at the hands of such a city; no subject complains that his masters are unworthy of him.   And we shall assuredly not be without witnesses; there are mighty monuments of our power which will make us the wonder of this and of succeeding ages: we shall not need the praises of Homer or of any other panegyrist, whose poetry may please for the moment, although his representation of the facts will not bear the light of day.   For we have compelled every land, every sea, to open a path for our valour, and have everywhere planted eternal memorials of our friendship and of our enmity." [1]

An impression so superb as this it is almost a pity to mar with the inevitable complement of disaster and decay.   But our account of the Athenian polity would be misleading and incomplete if we did not indicate how the idea of equality, on which it turned, defeated itself, as did, in Sparta, the complementary idea of order, by the excesses of its own development.   Already before the close of the fifth century, and with reiterated emphasis in the earlier decades of the fourth, we hear from poets and orators praise

[1] Thuc. II. 37.—Translated by Jowett.

of a glorious past that is dead, and denunciations of a decadent present. The ancient training in gymnastics, we are told, the ancient and generous culture of mind and soul, is neglected and despised by a generation of traders; reverence for age and authority, even for law, has disappeared; and in the train of these have gone the virtues they engendered and nurtured. Cowardice has succeeded to courage, disorder to discipline; the place of the statesman is usurped by the demagogue; and instead of a nation of heroes, marshalled under the supremacy of the wise and good, modern Athens presents to view a disordered and competitive mob, bent only on turning each to his own personal advantage the now corrupt machinery of administration and law.

And however much exaggeration there may be in these denunciations and regrets, we know enough of the interior working of the institutions of Athens to see that she had to pay in license and in fraud the bitter price of equality and freedom. That to the influence of disinterested statesmen succeeded, as the democracy accentuated itself, the tyranny of unscrupulous demagogues, is evidenced by the testimony, not only of the enemies of popular government, but by that of a democrat so convinced as Demosthenes. "Since these orators have appeared," he says, "who ask, What is your pleasure? what shall I move? how can I oblige you? the public welfare is complimented away for a moment's popularity, and these are the results; the orators thrive, you are disgraced. . . . Anciently the people, having the courage to be soldiers, controlled the statesmen and disposed of all emoluments; any of the rest were happy to receive from the people his share of honour, office, or advantage. Now, contrariwise, the statesmen dispose of emoluments; through them everything is done; you, the people, enervated, stripped of treasure and allies, are become as underlings and hangers-on, happy if these persons dole you out show-money or send you paltry beeves; and, the unmanliest part of all, you are grateful for receiving your own." [1]

And this indictment is amply confirmed from other sources. We know that the populace was demoralized by payments from the public purse; that the fee for attendance in the Assembly attracted thither, as ready instruments in the hands of ambitious men, the poorest and most degraded of the citizens; that the fees of jurors were a not unimportant addition to the income of an indigent class, who had thus a direct interest in the multiplication of suits; and that the city was infested by a race of "sycophants," whose profession was to manufacture frivolous and vexatious indictments. Of one of these men Demosthenes speaks as follows:

"He cannot show any respectable or honest employment in which his life is engaged. His mind is not occupied in promoting any political good: he attends not to any trade, or husbandry, or other business; he is connected with no one by ties of humanity or social union: but he walks through the market-

[1] Dem. Ol. III.—Translation by Kennedy.

place like a viper or a scorpion, with his sting up-
lifted, hastening here and there, and looking out for
someone whom he may bring into a scrape, or fasten
some calumny or mischief upon, and put in alarm in
order to extort money." [1]

From all this we may gather an idea of the way
in which the Athenian democracy by its own development destroyed itself. Beginning, on its first
emergence from an earlier aristocratic phase, with
an energy that inspired without shattering the forms
of discipline and law, it dissolved by degrees this
coherent whole into an anarchy of individual wills,
drawn deeper and deeper, in pursuit of mean and
egoistic ends, into political fraud and commercial
chicanery, till the tradition of the gentleman and
the soldier was choked by the dust of adventurers
and swindlers, and the people, whose fathers had
fought and prevailed at Marathon and Salamis, fell
as they deserved, by treachery from within as much
as by force from without, into the grasp of the
Macedonian conqueror.

§ 11. SCEPTICAL CRITICISM OF THE BASIS OF
THE STATE

Having thus supplemented our general account of
the Greek conception of the state by a description
of their two most prominent polities, it remains for
us in conclusion briefly to trace the negative criticism

[1] Demosth. in Aristogeit. A. 62.—Translation by Kennedy.

under whose attack that conception threatened to dissolve.

We have quoted, in an earlier part of this chapter, a striking passage from Demosthenes, embodying that view of the objective validity of law under which alone political institutions can be secure. "That is law," said the orator, "which all men ought to obey for many reasons, and especially because every law is an invention and gift of the gods, a resolution of wise men, a correction of errors intentional and unintentional, a compact of the whole state, according to which all who belong to the state ought to live." That is the conception of law which the citizens of any stable state must be prepared substantially to accept, for it is the condition of that fundamental belief in established institutions which alone can make it worth while to adapt and to improve them. It was, accordingly, the conception tacitly, at least, accepted in Greece, during the period of her constructive vigour. But it is a conception constantly open to attack. For law, at any given moment, even under the most favourable conditions, cannot do more than approximate to its own ideal. It is, at best, but a rough attempt at that reconciliation of conflicting interests towards which the reason of mankind is always seeking; and even in well-ordered states there must always be individuals and classes who resent, and rightly resent it, as unjust. But the Greek states, as we have seen, were not well ordered; on the contrary, they were always on the verge, or in the act, of civil war; and the conception of law, as "a compact of the whole state, according to which all who belong to the state ought to live," must have been, at the least, severely tried, in cities permanently divided into two factions, each intent not merely on defeating the other, but on excluding it altogether from political rights.   Such conditions, in fact, must have irresistibly suggested the criticism, which always dogs the idea of the state, and against which its only defence is in a perpetual perfection of itself—the criticism that law, after all, is only the rule of the strong, and justice the name under which they gloze their usurpation.   That is a point of view which, even apart from their political dissensions, would hardly have escaped the subtle intellect of the Greeks; and, in fact, from the close of the fifth century onwards, we find it constantly canvassed and discussed.

The mind of Plato, in particular, was exercised by this contention; and it was, one may say, a main object of his teaching to rescue the idea of justice from identification with the special interest of the strong, and re-affirm it as the general interest of all. For this end, he takes occasion to state, with the utmost frankness and lucidity, the view which it is his intention to refute; and consequently it is in his works that we find the fullest exposition of the destructive argument he seeks to answer.

Briefly, that argument runs as follows: It is the law of nature that the strong shall rule; a law which everyone recognizes in fact, though everyone repudiates it in theory. Government therefore simply means the rule of the strong, and exists, no matter what its form, whether tyranny, oligarchy, or democracy, in the interests not of its subjects but of itself. "Justice" and "law" are the specious names it employs to cloak its own arbitrary will; they have no objective validity, no reference to the well-being of all; and it is only the weak and the foolish on whom they impose. Strong and original natures sweep away this tangle of words, assert themselves in defiance of false shame, and claim the right divine that is theirs by nature, to rule at their will by virtue of their strength. "Each government," says Thrasymachus in the Republic, "has its laws framed to suit its own interests; a democracy making democratic laws; an autocrat despotic laws, and so on. Now by this procedure these governments have pronounced that what is for the interest of themselves is just for their subjects; and whoever deviates from this, is chastized by them as guilty of illegality and injustice. Therefore, my good sir, my meaning is, that in all cities the same thing, namely, the interest of the established government is just. And superior strength, I presume, is to be found on the side of government. So that the conclusion of right reasoning is, that the same thing, namely, the interest of the stronger, is everywhere just." [1]

Here is an argument which strikes at the root of all subordination to the state, setting the subject against the ruler, the minority against the majority, with an emphasis of opposition that admits of no conceivable reconciliation. And, as we have noticed, it was an argument to which the actual politi-

[1] Plato, Rep. 338.—Translated by Davies and Vaughan.

cal conditions of Greece gave a strong show of
plausibility.

How then did the constructive thinkers of Greece
attempt to meet it?

The procedure adopted by Plato is curiously opposed to that which might seem natural to a modern
thinker on politics. The scepticism which was to
be met, having sprung from the extremity of class-
antagonism, it might be supposed that the cure would
be sought in some sort of system of equality.
Plato's idea is precisely the contrary. The distinction between classes he exaggerates to its highest
point; only he would have it depend on degrees,
not of wealth, but of excellence. In the ideal republic which he constructs as a type of a state where
justice should really rule, he sets an impassable gulf
between the governing class and the governed; each
is specially trained and specially bred for its appropriate function; and the harmony between them is
ensured by the recognition, on either part, that each
is in occupation of the place for which it is naturally
fitted in that whole to which both, alike are subordinate. Such a state, no doubt, if ever it had been
realized in practice, would have been a complete
reply to the sceptical argument; for it would have
established a "justice" which was the expression not
of the caprice of the governing class, but of the objective will of the whole community. But in practice such a state was not realized in Greece; and
the experience of the Greek world does not lead us
to suppose that it was capable of realization. The
system of sterotyping classes—in a word, of caste—

which has played so great a part in the history of the
world, does no doubt embody a great truth, that of
natural inequality; and this truth, as we saw, was
at the bottom of that Greek conception of the state,
of which the "Republic" of Plato is an idealizing
caricature. But the problem is to make the inequality of nature really correspond to the inequality
imposed by institutions. This problem Plato hoped
to solve by a strict public control of the marriage relation, so that none should be born into any class
who were not naturally fitted to be members of it;
but, as a matter of fact, the difficulty has never been
met; and the system of caste remains open to the
reproach that its "justice" is conventional and arbitrary, not the expression of the objective nature and
will of all classes and members of the community.

The attempt of Aristotle to construct a state that
should be the embodiment of justice is similar to
Plato's so far as the relation of classes is concerned.
He, too, postulates a governing class of soldiers and
councillors, and a subject class of productive labourers. When, however, he turns from the ideal to
practical politics, and considers merely how to avoid
the worst extremes of party antagonism, his solution
is the simple and familiar one of the preponderance
of the middle class. The same view was dominant
both in French and English politics from the year
1830 onwards, and is only now being thrust aside by
the democratic ideal. In Greece it was never realized except as a passing phase in the perpetual flux
of polities. And in fine it may be said that the
problem of establishing a state which should be a

concrete refutation of the sceptical criticism that
"justice" is merely another name for force, was one
that was never solved in ancient Greece.   The dissolution of the idea of the state was more a symptom
than a cause of its failure in practice to harmonize
its warring elements.   And Greece, divided into conflicting polities, each of which again was divided
within itself, passed on to Macedon and thence to
Rome that task of reconciling the individual and the
class with the whole, about which the political history of the world turns.

§ 12. SUMMARY

We have now given some account of the general
character of the Greek state, the ideas that underlay
it, and the criticism of those ideas suggested by the
course of history and formulated by speculative
thought.   It remains to offer certain reflections on
the political achievement of the Greeks, and its relation to our own ideas.

The fruitful and positive aspect of the Greek
state, that which fastens upon it the eyes of later
generations as upon a model, if not to be copied, at
least to be praised and admired, is that identification of the individual citizen with the corporate life,
which delivered him from the narrow circle of personal interests into a sphere of wider views and
higher aims.   The Greek citizen, as we have seen, in
the best days of the best states, in Athens for example in the age of Pericles, was at once a soldier
and a politician; body and mind alike were at his

country's service; and his whole ideal of conduct was inextricably bound up with his intimate and personal participation in public affairs. If now with this ideal we contrast the life of an average citizen in a modern state, the absorption in private business and family concerns, the "greasy domesticity" (to use a phrase of Byron's), that limits and clouds his vision of the world, we may well feel that the Greeks had achieved something which we have lost, and may even desire to return, so far as we may, upon our steps, and to re-establish that interpenetration of private and public life by which the individual citizen was at once depressed and glorified.

It may be doubted, however, whether such a procedure would be in any way possible or desirable. For in the first place, the existence of the Greek citizen depended upon that of an inferior class who were regarded not as ends in themselves, but as means to his perfection. And that is an arrangement which runs directly counter to the modern ideal. All modern societies aim, to this extent at least, at equality, that their tendency, so far as it is conscious and avowed, is not to separate off a privileged class of citizens, set free by the labour of others to live the perfect life, but rather to distribute impartially to all the burdens and advantages of the state, so that every one shall be at once a labourer for himself and a citizen of the state. But this ideal is clearly incompatible with the Greek conception of the citizen. It implies that the greater portion of every man's life must be devoted to some kind of mechanical labour, whose immediate connection with the public good, though certain, is remote and obscure; and that in consequence a deliberate and unceasing preoccupation with the end of the state becomes as a general rule impossible.

And, in the second place, the mere complexity and size of a modern state is against the identification of the man with the citizen. For, on the one hand, public issues are so large and so involved that it is only a few who can hope to have any adequate comprehension of them; and on the other, the subdivision of functions is so minute that even when a man is directly employed in the service of the state his activity is confined to some highly specialized department. He must choose, for example, whether he will be a clerk in the treasury or a soldier; but he cannot certainly be both. In the Greek state any citizen could undertake, simultaneously or in succession, and with complete comprehension and mastery, every one of the comparatively few and simple public offices; in a modern state such an arrangement has become impossible. The mere mechanical and physical conditions of our life preclude the ideal of the ancient citizen.

But, it may be said, the activity of the citizen of a modern state should be and increasingly will be concerned not with the whole but with the part. By the development of local institutions he will come, more and more, to identify himself with the public life of his district and his town; and will bear to that much the same relation as was borne by the ancient Greek to his city-state. Certainly so far as the limitation of area and the simplicity and intelligibility of issues is concerned, such an analogy might be fairly pressed; and it is probably in connection with such local areas that the average citizen does and increasingly will become aware of his corporate relations. But, on the other hand, it can hardly be maintained that public business in this restricted sense either could or should play the part in the life of the modern man that it played in that of the ancient Greek. For local business after all is a matter of sewers and parks; and however great the importance of such matters may be, and however great their claim upon the attention of competent men, yet the kind of interest they awaken and the kind of faculties they employ can hardly be such as to lead to the identification of the individual ideal with that of public activity. The life of the Greek citizen involved an exercise, the finest and most complete, of all his powers of body, soul, and mind; the same can hardly be said of the life of a county councillor, even of the best and most conscientious of them. And the conclusion appears to be, that that fusion of public and private life which was involved in the ideal of the Greek citizen, was a passing phase in the history of the world; that the state can never occupy again the place in relation to the individual which it held in the cities of the ancient world; and that an attempt to identify in a modern state the ideal of the man with that of the citizen, would be an historical anachronism.

Nor is this a conclusion which need be regretted. For as the sphere of the state shrinks, it is possible that that of the individual may be enlarged. The public side of human life, it may be supposed, will become more and more mechanical, as our understanding and control of social forces grow. But every reduction to habit and rule of what were once spiritual functions, implies the liberation of the higher powers for a possible activity in other regions. And if advantage were taken of this opportunity, the inestimable compensation for the contraction to routine of the life of the citizen would be the expansion into new spheres of speculation and passion of the freer and more individual life of the man.

CHAPTER III

THE GREEK VIEW OF THE INDIVIDUAL

§ 1. THE GREEK VIEW OF MANUAL LABOUR AND TRADE

IN our discussion of the Greek view of the state we noticed the tendency both of the theory and the practice of the Greeks to separate the citizens proper from the rest of the community as a distinct and aristocratic class. And this tendency, we had occasion to observe, was partly to be attributed to the high conception which the Greeks had formed of the proper excellence of man, an excellence which it was the function of the citizen to realize in his own person, at the cost, if need be, of the other members of the state. This Greek conception of the proper excellence of man it is now our purpose to examine more closely.

The chief point that strikes us about the Greek ideal is its comprehensiveness. Our own word "virtue" is applied only to moral qualities; but the Greek word which we so translate should properly be rendered "excellence," and includes a reference to the body as well as to the soul. A beautiful soul, housed in a beautiful body, and supplied with all the external advantages necessary to produce and perpetrate such a combination—that is the Greek

137

conception of well-being; and it is because labour
with the hands or at the desk distorts or impairs the
body, and the petty cares of a calling pursued for
bread pervert the soul, that so strong a contempt
was felt by the Greeks for manual labour and trade.
"The arts that are called mechanical," says Xenophon, "are also, and naturally enough, held in bad
repute in our cities. For they spoil the bodies of
workers and superintendents alike, compelling them
to live sedentary indoor lives, and in some cases
even to pass their days by the fire. And as their
bodies become effeminate, so do their souls also grow
less robust. Besides this, in such trades one has no
leisure to devote to the care of one's friends or of
one's city. So that those who engage in them are
thought to be bad backers of their friends and bad
defenders of their country." [1]   In a similar spirit
Plato asserts that a life of drudgery disfigures the
body and mars and enervates the soul; [2] while Aristotle defines a mechanical trade as one which
"renders the body and soul or intellect of free persons unfit for the exercise and practice of virtue;" [3]
and denies to the artisan not merely the proper
excellence of man, but any excellence of any kind,
on the plea that his occupation and status is unnatural, and that he misses even that reflex of human virtue which a slave derives from his intimate
connection with his master.[4]

[1] Xen. Oec. IV. 3.
[2] Plato, Rep. 495.
[3] Arist. Pol. V. 1337 b 8.—Translated by Welldon.
[4] *Ibid.* I. 1260 a 34.

If, then, the artisan was excluded from the citizenship in some of the Greek states, and even in the most democratic of them never altogether threw off the stigma of inferiority attaching to his trade, the reason was that the life he was compelled to lead was incompatible with the Greek conception of excellence. That conception we will now proceed to examine a little more in detail.

§ 2. APPRECIATION OF EXTERNAL GOODS

In the first place, the Greek ideal required for its realization a solid basis of external Goods. It recognized frankly the dependence of man upon the world of sense, and the contribution to his happiness of elements over which he had at best but a partial control. Not that it placed his Good outside himself, in riches, power, and other such appendages; but that it postulated certain gifts of fortune as necessary means to his self-development. Of these the chief were, a competence, to secure him against sordid cares, health, to ensure his physical excellence, and children, to support and protect him in old age. Aristotle's definition of the happy man is "one whose activity accords with perfect virtue and who is adequately furnished with external goods, not for a casual period of time but for a complete or perfect life-time;" [1] and he remarks, somewhat caustically, that those who say

[1] Arist. Ethics. I. 11. 1101 a 14.—Translated by Welldon.

that a man on the rack would be happy if only
he were good, intentionally or unintentionally are
talking nonsense. That here, as elsewhere, Aristotle
represents the common Greek view we have abund-
ant testimony from other sources. Even Plato,
in whom there runs so clear a vein of asceticism,
follows the popular judgment in reckoning high
among Goods, first, health, then beauty, then skill
and strength in physical exercises, and lastly wealth,
if it be not blind but illumined by the eye of reason.
To these Goods must be added, to complete the
scale, success and reputation, topics which are the
constant theme of the poets' eulogy. "Two things
alone there are," says Pindar, "that cherish life's
bloom to its utmost sweetness amidst the fair
flowers of wealth—to have good success and to win
therefore fair fame;" [1] and the passage represents
his habitual attitude. That the gifts of fortune,
both personal and external, are an essential condition of excellence, is an axiom of the point of view
of the Greeks. But on the other hand we never
find them misled into the conception that such gifts
are an end in themselves, apart from the personal
qualities they are meant to support or adorn. The
oriental ideal of unlimited wealth and power, enjoyed merely for its own sake, never appealed to
their fine and lucid judgment. Nothing could
better illustrate this point than the anecdote related by Herodotus of the interview between Solon
and Crœsus, King of Lydia. Crœsus, proud of

[1] Pind. Isth. IV. 14.—Translated by E. Myers.

his boundless wealth, asks the Greek stranger who is the happiest man on earth? expecting to hear in reply his own name. Solon, however, answers with the name of Tellus, the Athenian, giving his reasons in the following speech:

"First, because his country was flourishing in his days, and he himself had sons both beautiful and good, and he lived to see children born to each of them, and these children all grew up; and further because, after a life spent in what our people look upon as comfort, his end was surpassingly glorious. In a battle between the Athenians and their neighbours near Eleusis, he came to the assistance of his countrymen, routed the foe, and died upon the field most gallantly. The Athenians gave him a public funeral on the spot where he fell, and paid him the highest honours."

Later on in the discussion Solon defines the happy man as he who "is whole of limb, a stranger to disease, free from misfortune, happy in his children, and comely to look upon," and who also ends his life well.[1]

§ 3. APPRECIATION OF PHYSICAL QUALITIES

While, however, the gifts of a happy fortune are an essential condition of the Greek ideal, they are not to be mistaken for the ideal itself. "A beautiful soul in a beautiful body," to recur to our former phrase, is the real end and aim of their

[1] Herodotus, I. 30. 32.—Translated by Rawlinson.

endeavour. "Beautiful and good" is their habitual way of describing what we should call a gentleman; and no expression could better represent what they admired. With ourselves, in spite of our addiction to athletics, the body takes a secondary place; after a certain age, at least, there are few men who make its systematic cultivation an important factor of their life; and in our estimate of merit physical qualities are accorded either none or the very smallest weight. It was otherwise with the Greeks; to them a good body was the necessary correlative of a good soul. Balance was what they aimed at, balance and harmony; and they could scarcely believe in the beauty of the spirit, unless it were reflected in the beauty of the flesh. The point is well put by Plato, the most spiritually minded of the Greeks, and the least apt to under-prize the qualities of the soul.

"Surely then," he says, "to him who has an eye to see, there can be no fairer spectacle than that of a man who combines the possession of moral beauty in his soul with outward beauty of form, corresponding and harmonizing with the former, because the same great pattern enters into both.

"There can be none so fair.

"And you will grant that what is fairest is loveliest?

"Undoubtedly it is.

"Then the truly musical person will love those who combine most perfectly moral and physical beauty, but will not love any one in whom there is dissonance.

"No, not if there be any defect in the soul, but if it is only a bodily blemish, he may so bear with it as to be willing to regard it with complacency.

"I understand that you have now, or have had, a favourite of this kind; so I give way." [1]

The reluctance of the admission that a physical defect may possibly be overlooked is as significant as the rest of the passage. Body and soul, it is clear, are regarded as aspects of a single whole, so that a blemish in the one indicates and involves a blemish in the other. The training of the body is thus, in a sense, the training of the soul, and gymnastic and music, as Plato puts it, serve the same end, the production of a harmonious temperament.

§ 4. GREEK ATHLETICS

It is this conception which gives, or appears at least in the retrospect to give, a character so gracious and fine to Greek athletics. In fact, if we look more closely into the character of the public games in Greece we see that they were so surrounded and transfused by an atmosphere of imagination that their appeal must have been as much to the æsthetic as to the physical sense. For in the first place those great gymnastic contests in which all Hellas took part, and which gave the tone to their whole athletic life, were primarily religious festivals. The Olympic and Nemean

[1] Plato, Rep. 402.—Translated by Davies and Vaughan.

Games were held in honour of Zeus, the Pythian, of Apollo, the Isthmean, of Poseidon. In the enclosures in which they took place stood temples of the gods; and sacrifice, prayer, and choral hymn were the background against which they were set. And since in Greece religion implied art, in the wake of the athlete followed the sculptor and the poet. The colossal Zeus of Pheidias, the wonder of the ancient world, flashed from the precincts of Olympia its glory of ivory and gold; temples and statues broke the brilliant light into colour and form; and under that vibrating heaven of beauty, the loveliest nature crowned with the finest art, shifted and shone what was in itself a perfect type of both, the grace of harmonious motion in naked youths and men. For in Greek athletics, by virtue of the practice of contending nude, the contest itself became a work of art; and not only did sculptors draw from it an inspiration such as has been felt by no later age, but to the combatants themselves, and the spectators, the plastic beauty of the human form grew to be more than its prowess or its strength, and gymnastic became a training in æsthetics as much as, or more than, in physical excellence.

And as with the contest, so with the reward, everything was designed to appeal to the sensuous imagination. The prize formally adjudged was symbolical only, a crown of olive; but the real triumph of the victor was the ode in which his praise was sung, the procession of happy comrades, and the evening festival, when, as Pindar has it, "the lovely shining of the fair-faced moon beamed forth, and all the precinct sounded with songs of festal glee," [1] or "beside Kastaly in the evening his name burnt bright, when the glad sounds of the Graces rose." [2]

Of the Graces! for these were the powers who presided over the world of Greek athletics. Here, for example, is the opening of one of Pindar's odes, typical of the spirit in which he at least conceived the functions of the chronicler of sport:

"O ye who haunt the land of goodly steeds that drinketh of Kephisos' waters, lusty Orchomenos' Queens renowned in song, O Graces, guardians of the Minyai's ancient race, hearken, for unto you I pray. For by your gift come unto men all pleasant things and sweet, and the wisdom of a man and his beauty, and the splendour of his fame. Yea, even gods without the Graces' aid rule never at feast or dance; but these have charge of all things done in heaven, and beside Pythian Apollo of the golden bow they have set their thrones, and worship the eternal majesty of the Olympian Father. O lady Aglaia, and thou Euphrosyne, lover of song, children of the mightiest of the gods, listen and hear, and thou Thalia, delighting in sweet sounds, and look down upon this triumphal company, moving with light step under happy fate. In Lydian mood

---

[1] Pindar, Ol. XI. 90.—Translated by Myers.
[2] Pindar, Nem. VI. 65.

of melody concerning Asopichos am I come hither
to sing, for that through thee, Aglaia, in the Olympic
games the Minyai's home is winner." [1]

This is but a single passage among many that
might be quoted to illustrate the point we are endeavouring to bring into relief—the conscious predominance in the Greek games of that element of
poetry and art which is either not present at all in
modern sport or at best is a happy accessory of
chance. The modern man, and especially the
Englishman, addicts himself to athletics, as to
other avocations, with a certain stolidity of gaze
on the immediate end which tends to confine him to
the purely physical view of his pursuit. The Greek,
an artist by nature, lifted his not less strenuous
sports into an air of finer sentiment, touched them
with the poetry of legend and the grace of art and
song, and even to his most brutal contests—for
brutal some of them were—imparted so rich an
atmosphere of beauty, that they could be admitted
as fit themes for dedication to the Graces by the
choice and spiritual genius of Pindar.

§ 5. Greek Ethics—Identification of the Æsthetic and Ethical Points of View

And as with the excellence of the body, so with
that of the soul, the conception that dominated the
mind of the Greeks was primarily æsthetic. In
speaking of their religion we have already remarked

[1] Pindar, Ol. XIV.—Translated by Myers

that they had no sense of sin; and we may now add that they had not what we are apt to mean by a sense of duty. Moral virtue they conceived not as obedience to an external law, a sacrifice of the natural man to a power that in a sense is alien to himself, but rather as the tempering into due proportion of the elements of which human nature is composed. The good man was the man who was beautiful—beautiful in soul. "Virtue," says Plato, "will be a kind of health and beauty and good habit of the soul; and vice will be a disease and deformity and sickness of it."[1] It follows that it is as natural to seek virtue and to avoid vice as to seek health and to avoid disease. There is no question of a struggle between opposite principles; the distinction of good and evil is one of order or confusion, among elements which in themselves are neither good nor bad.

This conception of virtue we find expressed in many forms, but always with the same underlying idea. A favourite watchword with the Greeks is the "middle" or "mean," the exact point of rightness between two extremes. "Nothing in excess," was a motto inscribed over the temple of Delphi; and none could be more characteristic of the ideal of these lovers of proportion. Aristotle, indeed, has made it the basis of his whole theory of ethics. In his conception, virtue is the mean, vice the excess lying on either side—courage, for example, the mean between foolhardiness and cowardice, tem-

[1] Plato, Rep. 444.—Translated by Davies and Vaughan.

perance, between incontinence and insensibility, generosity, between extravagance and meanness. The various phases of feeling and the various kinds of action he analyzes minutely on this principle, understanding always by "the mean" that which adapts itself in the due proportion to the circumstances and requirements of every case.

The interest of this view for us lies in its assumption that it is not passions or desires in themselves that must be regarded as bad, but only their disproportional or misdirected indulgence. Let us take, for example, the case of the pleasures of sense. The puritan's rule is to abjure them altogether; to him they are absolutely wrong in themselves, apart from all considerations of time and place. Aristotle, on the contrary, enjoins not renunciation but temperance; and defines the temperate man as one who "holds a mean position in respect of pleasures. He takes no pleasure in the things in which the licentious man takes most pleasure; he rather dislikes them; nor does he take pleasure at all in wrong things, nor an excessive pleasure in anything that is pleasant, nor is he pained at the absence of such things, nor does he desire them, except perhaps in moderation, nor does he desire them more than is right, or at the wrong time, and so on. But he will be eager in a moderate and right spirit for all such things as are pleasant and at the same time conducive to health or to a sound bodily condition, and for all other pleasures, so long as they are not prejudicial to these or inconsistent with noble conduct or extravagant beyond his means.

For unless a person limits himself in this way, he affects such pleasures more than is right, whereas the temperate man follows the guidance of right reason." [1]

As another illustration of this point of view, we may take the case of anger. The Christian rule is never to resent an injury, but rather, in the New Testament phrase, to "turn the other cheek." Aristotle, while blaming the man who is unduly passionate, blames equally the man who is insensitive; the thing to aim at is to be angry "on the proper occasions and with the proper people in the proper manner and for the proper length of time." And in this and all other cases the definition of what is proper must be left to the determination of "the sensible man."

Thus, in place of a series of hard and fast rules, a rigid and uncompromising distinction of acts and affections into good and bad, the former to be absolutely chosen and the latter absolutely eschewed, Aristotle presents us with the general type of a subtle and shifting problem, the solution of which must be worked out afresh by each individual in each particular case. Conduct to him is a free and living creature, and not a machine controlled by fixed laws. Every life is a work of art shaped by the man who lives it; according to the faculty of the artist will be the quality of his work, and no general rules can supply the place of his own direct

[1] Arist. Ethics. III. 14.—1119 a 11.—Translated by Welldon.

perception at every turn. The Good is the right proportion, the right manner and occasion; the Bad is all that varies from this "right." But the elements of human nature in themselves are neither good nor bad; they are merely the raw material out of which the one or the other may be shaped.

The idea thus formulated by Aristotle is typically Greek. In another form it is the basis of the ethical philosophy of Plato, who habitually regards virtue as a kind of "order." "The virtue of each thing," he says, "whether body or soul, instrument or creature, when given to them in the best way comes to them not by chance, but as the result of the order and truth and art which are imparted to them." [1] And the conception here indicated is worked out in detail in his Republic. There, after distinguishing in the soul three principles or powers, reason, passion, and desire, he defines justice as the maintenance among them of their proper mutual relation, each moving in its own place and doing its appropriate work as is, or should be, the case with the different classes in a state.

"The just man will not permit the several principles within him to do any work but their own, nor allow the distinct classes in his soul to interfere with each other, but will really set his house in order; and having gained the mastery over himself, will so regulate his own character as to be on good terms with himself, and to set those three principles in tune together, as if they were verily three

[1] Plato, Gorgias, 506 d.—Translated by Jowett.

cords of a harmony, a higher and a lower and a
middle, and whatever may lie between these; and
after he has bound all these together, and reduced
the many elements of his nature to a real unity,
as a temperate and duly harmonized man, he will
then at length proceed to do whatever he may have
to do." [1]

Plato, it is true, in other parts of his work,
approaches more closely to the dualistic conception
of an absolute opposition between good and bad
principles in man. Yet even so, he never altogether
abandons that æsthetic point of view which looks
to the establishment of order among the conflicting principles rather than to the annihilation of one
by the other in an internecine conflict. The point
may be illustrated by the following passage, where
the two horses represent respectively the elements
of fleshly desire and spiritual passion, while the
charioteer stands for the controlling reason; and
where, it will be noticed, the ultimate harmony is
achieved, not by the complete eradication of desire,
but by its due subordination to the higher principle.
Even Plato the most ascetic of the Greeks, is a
Greek first and an ascetic afterwards.

"Of the nature of the soul, though her true form
be ever a theme of large and more than mortal
discourse, let me speak briefly, and in a figure,
and let the figure be composite—a pair of winged
horses and a charioteer. Now the winged horses

[1] Plato, Rep. IV. 443.—Translation by Davies and
Vaughan.

and the charioteers of the gods are all of them
noble and of noble descent, but those of other races
are mixed; the human charioteer drives his in a
pair; and one of them is noble and of noble breed,
and the other is ignoble and of ignoble breed; and
the driving of them of necessity gives a great deal
of trouble to him. . . . The right-hand horse is
upright and cleanly made; he has a lofty neck and
an aquiline nose; his colour is white, and his eyes
dark; he is a lover of honour and modesty and
temperance, and the follower of true glory; he needs
no touch of the whip, but is guided by word and
admonition only.   The other is a crooked lumbering
animal, put together anyhow; he has a short thick
neck; he is flat-faced and of a dark colour, with
grey eyes and blood-red complexion; the mate of
insolence and pride, shag-eared and deaf, hardly
yielding to whip and spur. Now when the
charioteer beholds the vision of love, and has his
whole soul warmed through sense, and is full of the
pricklings and ticklings of desire, the obedient
steed, then as always under the government of
shame, refrains from leaping on the beloved; but the
other, heedless of the blows of the whip, plunges
and runs away, giving all manner of trouble to his
companion and the charioteer, whom he forces to
approach the beloved and to remember the joys
of love. They at first indignantly oppose him and
will not be urged on to do terrible and unlawful
deeds; but at last, when he persists in plaguing
them, they yield and agree to do as he bids them.

And now they are at the spot and behold the flashing beauty of the beloved; which when the charioteer sees, his memory is carried to the true beauty whom he beholds in company with Modesty like an image placed upon a holy pedestal. He sees her, but he is afraid and falls backwards in adoration, and by his fall is compelled to pull back the reins with such violence as to bring both the steeds on their haunches, the one willing and unresisting, the unruly one very unwilling; and when they have gone back a little, the one is overcome with shame and wonder, and his whole soul is bathed in perspiration; the other, when the pain is over which the bridle and the fall had given him, having with difficulty taken breath, is full of wrath and reproaches, which he heaps upon the charioteer and his fellow-steed, for want of courage and manhood, declaring that they have been false to their agreement and guilty of desertion. Again they refuse, and again he urges them on, and will scarce yield to their prayer that he would wait until another time. When the appointed hour comes, they make as if they had forgotten, and he reminds them, fighting and neighing and dragging them on, until at length he on the same thoughts intent, forces them to draw near again. And when they are near he stoops his head and puts up his tail, and takes the bit in his teeth and pulls shamelessly. Then the charioteer is worse off than ever; he falls back like a racer at the barrier, and with a still more violent wrench drags the bit out of the teeth of the wild steed and covers his abusive jaws and tongue with blood, and forces his legs and haunches to the ground and punishes him sorely.

"And when this has happened several times, and the villain has ceased from his wanton way, he is tamed and humbled, and follows the will of the charioteer, and when he sees the beautiful one he is ready to die of fear. And from that time forward the soul of the lover follows the beloved in modesty and holy fear." [1]

Even from this passage, in spite of its dualistic hypothesis, but far more clearly from the whole tenor of his work, we may perceive that Plato's description of virtue as an "order" of the soul is prompted by the same conception, characteristically Greek, as Aristotle's account of virtue as a "mean." The view, as we said at the beginning, is properly æsthetic rather than moral. It regards life less as a battle between two contending principles, in which victory means the annihilation of the one, the altogether bad, by the other, the altogether good, than as the maintenance of a balance between elements neutral in themselves but capable, according as their relations are rightly ordered or the reverse, of producing either that harmony which is called virtue, or that discord which is called vice.

Such being the conception of virtue characteristic of the Greeks, it follows that the motive to pursue it can hardly have presented itself to them in the form of what we call the "sense of duty."

[1] Plato, Phaedrus. 246.—Translated by Jowett.

For duty emphasizes self-repression. Against the
desires of man it sets a law of prohibition, a law
which is not conceived as that of his own complete nature, asserting against a partial or dispro-
portioned development the balance and totality of
the ideal, but rather as a rule imposed from without by a power distinct from himself, for the mortification, not the perfecting, of his natural impulses
and aims. Duty emphasizes self-repression; the
Greek view emphasized self-development. That
"health and beauty and good habit of the soul,"
which is Plato's ideal, is as much its own recom-
mendation to the natural man as is the health and
beauty of the body. Vice, on this view, is condemned because it is a frustration of nature, virtue
praised because it is her fulfilment; and the motive
throughout is simply that passion to realize oneself which is commonly acknowledged as sufficient
in the case of physical development and which
appeared sufficient to the Greeks in the case of the
development of the soul.

§ 6. The Greek View of Pleasure

From all this it follows clearly enough that the
Greek ideal was far removed from asceticism; but
it might perhaps be supposed, on the other hand,
that it came dangerously near to license. Nothing,
however, could be farther from the case. That
there were libertines among the Greeks, as everywhere else, goes without saying; but the conception that the Greek rule of life was to follow

impulse and abandon restraint is a figment of would-be "Hellenists" of our own time. The word which best sums up the ideal of the Greeks is "temperance"; "the mean," "order," "harmony," as we saw, are its characteristic expressions; and the self-realization to which they aspired was not an anarchy of passion, but an ordered evolution of the natural faculties under the strict control of a balanced mind. The point may be illustrated by a reference to the treatment of pleasure in the philosophy of Plato and of Aristotle.

The practice of the libertine is to identify pleasure and good in such a manner that he pursues at any moment any pleasure that presents itself, eschewing comparison and reflection, with all that might tend to check that continuous flow of vivid and fresh sensations which he postulates as the end of life. The ideal of the Greeks, on the contrary, as interpreted by their two greatest thinkers, while on the one hand it is so far opposed to asceticism that it requires pleasure as an essential complement of Good, on the other, is so far from identifying the two, that it recognizes an ordered scale of pleasures, and while rejecting altogether those at the lower end, admits the rest, not as in themselves constituting the Good, but rather as harmless additions, or at most as necessary accompaniments of its operation. Plato, in the Republic, distinguishes between the necessary and unnecessary pleasures, defining the former as those derived from the gratification of appetites "which we cannot get rid of, and whose satisfaction does

us good"—such, for example, as the appetite for
wholesome food; and the latter as those which belong to appetites "which we can put away from us
by early training; and the presence of which, besides, never does us any good, and in some cases
does positive harm"—such, for example, as the
appetite for delicate and luxurious dishes.[1] The
former he would admit, the latter he excludes from
his ideal of happiness. And though in a later
dialogue, the Philebus, he goes farther than this,
and would exclude from the perfect life all pleasures
except those which he describes as "pure," that is
those which attend upon the contemplation of form
and colour and sound, or which accompany intellectual activity; yet here, no doubt, he is passing beyond the sphere of the practicable ideal, and
his distinct personal bias towards asceticism must
be discounted if we are to take him as representative
of the Greek view. His general contention, however, that pleasures must be ranked as higher and
as lower, and that at the best they are not to be
identified with the Good, is fully accepted by so
typical a Greek as Aristotle. Aristotle, however,
is careful not to condemn any pleasure that is not
definitely harmful. Even "unnecessary" pleasures,
he admits, may be desirable in themselves; even
the deliberate creation of desire with a view to the
enjoyment of satisfying it may be admissible if it
is not injurious. Still, there are kinds of pleasures

[1] Plato, Rep. VIII. 558.—Translated by Davies and
Vaughan.

which ought not to be pursued, and occasions and
methods of seeking it which are improper and per-
verse. Therefore the Reason must be always at
hand to check and to control; and the ultimate test
of true worth in pleasure, as in everything else, is
the trained judgment of the good and sensible man.

§ 7. ILLUSTRATIONS—ISCHOMACHUS; SOCRATES

Such, then, was the character of the Greek conception of excellence. The account we have given
may seem somewhat abstract and ideal; but it gives
the general. formula of the life which every cultivated Greek would at any rate have wished to live.
And in confirmation of this point we may adduce
the testimony of Xenophon, who has left us a description, evidently drawn from life, of what he
conceives to be the perfect type of a "gentleman."
The interest of the account lies in the fact, that
Xenophon himself was clearly an "average" Greek,
one, that is to say, of good natural parts, of perfectly normal faculties and tastes, undisturbed by
any originality of character or mind, and representing, therefore, as we may fairly assert, the
ordinary views and aims of an upright and competent man of the world. His description of the
"gentleman," therefore, may be taken as a representative account of the recognized ideal of all that
class of Athenian citizens. And this is how the
gentleman in question, Ischomachus, describes his
course of life.

"In the first place," he says, "I worship the gods.

Next, I endeavour to the best of my ability, assisted by prayer, to get health and strength of body, reputation in the city, good will among my friends, honourable security in battle, and an honourable increase of fortune."

At this point Socrates, who is supposed to be the interlocutor, interrupts. "Do you really covet wealth," he asks, "with all the trouble it involves?" "Certainly I do," is the reply, "for it enables me to honour the gods magnificently, to help my friends if they are in want, and to contribute to the resources of my country."

Here definitely and precisely expressed is the ideal of the Athenian gentleman—the beautiful body housing the beautiful soul, the external aids of fortune, friends, and the like, and the realization of the individual self in public activity. Upon it follows an account of the way in which Ischomachus was accustomed to pass his days. He rises early, he tells us, to catch his friends before they go out, or walks to the city to transact his necessary business. If he is not called into town, he pays a visit to his farm, walking for the sake of exercise and sending on his horse. On his arrival he gives directions about the sowing, ploughing, or whatever it may be, and then mounting his horse practises his military exercises. Finally, he returns home on foot, running part of the way, takes his bath, and sits down to a moderate midday meal.

This combination of physical exercise, military training and business, arouses the enthusiasm of Socrates. "How right you are!" he cries, "and the

consequence is that you are as healthy and strong
as we see you, and one of the best riders and the
wealthiest men in the country!"

This little prosaic account of the daily life of an
Athenian gentleman is completely in harmony with
all we have said about the character of the Greek
ideal; but it comprehends only a part, and that the
least spiritual, of that rich and many-sided excellence. It may be as well, therefore, to append
by way of complement the description of another
personality, exceptional indeed even among the
Greeks, yet one which only Greece could have produced—the personality of Socrates. No more
striking figure is presented to us in history, none has
been more vividly portrayed, and none, in spite of
the originality of mind which provoked the hostility
of the crowd, is more thoroughly Hellenic in every
aspect, physical, intellectual, and moral.

That Socrates was ugly in countenance was a
defect which a Greek could not fail to note, and his
snub nose and big belly are matters of frequent and
jocose allusion. But apart from these defects his
physique, it appears, was exceptionally good; he
was sedulous in his attendance at the gymnasia, and
was noted for his powers of endurance and his
courage and skill in war. Plato records it of him
that in a hard winter on campaign, when the
common soldiers were muffling themselves in sheep-
skins and felt against the cold, he alone went about
in his ordinary cloak, and barefoot over the ice
and snow; and he further describes his bearing in
a retreat from a lost battle, how "there you might

see him, just as he is in the streets of Athens, stalking like a pelican and rolling his eyes, calmly contemplating enemies as well as friends, and making very intelligible to anybody, even from a distance, that whoever attacked him would be likely to meet with a stout resistance." [1]

To this efficiency of body corresponded, in accordance with the Greek ideal, a perfect balance and harmony of soul. Plato, in a fine figure, compares him to the wooden statues of Silenus, which concealed behind a grotesque exterior beautiful golden images of the gods. Of these divine forms none was fairer in Socrates than that typical Greek virtue, temperance. Without a touch of asceticism, he knew how to be contented with a little. His diet he measured strictly with a view to health. Naturally abstemious, he could drink, when he chose, more than another man; but no one had ever seen him drunk. His affections were strong and deep, but never led him away to seek his own gratification at the cost of those he loved. Without cutting himself off from any of the pleasures of life, a social man and a frequent guest at feasts, he preserved without an effort the supremacy of character and mind over the flesh he neither starved nor pampered. Here is a description by Plato of his bearing at the close of an all-night carouse, which may stand as a concrete illustration not only of the character of Socrates, but of the meaning of "temperance" as it was understood by the Greeks:

[1] Plato, Symp. 221 b.—Translated by Jowett.

"Aristodemus said that Eryximachus, Phædrus, and others went away—he himself fell asleep, and as the nights were long took a good rest: he was awakened towards daybreak by a crowing of cocks, and when he awoke the others were either asleep, or had gone away; there remained awake only Socrates, Aristophanes, and Agathon, who were drinking out of a large goblet which they passed round, and Socrates was discoursing to them. Aristodemus did not hear the beginning of the discourse, and he was only half awake, but the chief thing which he remembered was Socrates compelling the other two to acknowledge that the genius of comedy was the same as that of tragedy, and that the true artist in tragedy was an artist in comedy also. To this they assented, being drowsy, and not quite following the argument. And first of all Aristophanes dropped off, then, when the day was already dawning, Agathon. Socrates, when he had laid them to sleep, rose to depart; Aristodemus, as his manner was, following him. At the Lyceum he took a bath, and passed the day as usual. In the evening he retired to rest at his own house." [1]

With this quality of temperance was combined in Socrates a rare measure of independence and moral courage. He was never an active politician; but as every Athenian citizen was called, at some time or another, to public office, he found himself, on a critical occasion, responsible for putting a certain proposition to the vote in the Assembly. It

[1] Plato, Symposion, 223.—Translated by Jowett.

was a moment of intense excitement. A great victory had just been won; but the generals who had achieved the success had neglected to recover the corpses of the dead or save the shipwrecked. It was proposed to take a vote of life or death on all the generals collectively. Socrates, as it happened, was one of the committee whose duty it was to put the question to the Assembly. But the proposition was in itself illegal, and Socrates, with some other members of the committee, refused to submit it to the vote. Every kind of pressure was brought to bear upon the recalcitrant officers; orators threatened, friends besought, the mob clamoured and denounced. Finally, all but Socrates gave way. He alone, an old man, in office for the first time, had the courage to obey his conscience and the law in face of an angry populace crying for blood.

And as he could stand against a mob, so he could stand against a despot. At the time when Athens was ruled by the thirty tyrants he was ordered, with four others, to arrest a man whom the authorities wished to put out of the way. The man was guilty of no crime, and Socrates refused. "I went quietly home," he says, "and no doubt I should have been put to death for it, if the government had not shortly after come to an end."

These, however, were exceptional episodes in the career of a man who was never a prominent politician. The main interest of Socrates was intellectual and moral; an interest, however, rather practical than speculative. For though he was charged in his indictment with preaching atheism, he appears in fact to have concerned himself little or nothing with either theological or physical inquiries. He was careful in his observance of all prescribed religious rites, and probably accepted the gods as powers of the natural world and authors of human institutions and laws. His originality lay not in any purely speculative views, but in the pertinacious curiosity, practical in its origin and aim, with which he attacked and sifted the ethical conceptions of his time: "What is justice?" "What is piety?" "What is temperance?"—these were the kinds of questions he never tired of raising, pointing out contradictions and inconsistencies in current ideas, and awakening doubts which if negative in form were positive and fruitful in effect.

His method in pursuing these inquiries was that of cross-examination. In the streets, in the market, in the gymnasia, at meetings grave and gay, in season or out of season, he raised his points of definition. The city was in a ferment around him. Young men and boys followed and hung on his lips wherever he went. By the charm of his personality, his gracious courtesy and wit, and the large and generous atmosphere of a sympathy always at hand to temper to particular persons the rigours of a generalizing logic, he drew to himself, with a fascination not more of the intellect than of the heart, all that was best and brightest in the youth of Athens. His relation to his young disciples was that of a lover and a friend; and the stimulus given by his dialectics to their keen and

eager minds was supplemented and reinforced by
the appeal to their admiration and love of his sweet
and virile personality.

Only in Ancient Athens, perhaps, could such a
character and such conditions have met. The
sociable outdoor city life; the meeting places in the
open air, and especially the gymnasia, frequented
by young and old not more for exercise of the body
than for recreation of the mind, the nimble and
versatile Athenian wits trained to preternatural
acuteness by the debates of the law courts and the
Assembly; all this was exactly the environment
fitted to develop and sustain a genius at once so
subtle and so humane as that of Socrates. It is
the concrete presentation of this city-life that lends
so peculiar a charm to the dialogues of Plato. The
spirit of metaphysics puts on the human form; and
Dialectic walks the streets and contends in the
palæstra. It would be impossible to convey by
citation the cumulative effect of this constant reference in Plato to a human background; but a single
excerpt may perhaps help us to realize the conditions under which Socrates lived and worked. Here,
then, is a description of the scene in one of those
gymnasia in which he was wont to hold his conversations:

"Upon entering we found that the boys had just
been sacrificing; and this part of the festival was
nearly at an end. They were all in white array,
and games at dice were going on among them.
Most of them were in the outer court amusing themselves; but some were in a corner of the Apody-

terium playing at odd and even with a number of dice, which they took out of little wicker baskets. There was also a circle of lookers-on, one of whom was Lysis. He was standing among the other boys and youths, having a crown upon his head, like a fair vision, and not less worthy of praise for his goodness than for his beauty. We left them, and went over to the opposite side of the room, where, finding a quiet place, we sat down; and then we began to talk. This attracted Lysis, who was constantly turning round to look at us—he was evidently wanting to come to us. For a time he hesitated and had not the courage to come alone; but first of all, his friend Menexenus came in out of the court in the interval of his play, and when he saw Ctesippus and myself, came and sat by us; and then Lysis, seeing him, followed, and sat down with him, and the other boys joined.

"I turned to Menexenus, and said: 'Son of Demophon, which of you two youths is the elder?'

" 'That is a matter of dispute between us,' he said.

" 'And which is the nobler? Is that a matter of dispute too?'

" 'Yes, certainly.'

" 'And another disputed point is, which is the fairer?'

"The two boys laughed.

" 'I shall not ask which is the richer,' I said: 'for you two are friends, are you not?'

" 'Certainly,' they replied.

" 'And friends have all things in common, so that

one of you can be no richer than the other, if you say truly that you are friends.'

"They assented. I was about to ask which was the greater of the two, and which was the wiser of the two; but at this moment Menexenus was called away by some one who came and said that the gymnastic-master wanted him. I supposed that he had to offer sacrifice. So he went away and I asked Lysis some more questions." [1]

Such were the scenes in which Socrates passed his life. Of his influence it is hardly necessary here to speak at length. In the well-known metaphor put into his mouth by Plato, he was the "gad-fly" of the Athenian people. To prick intellectual lethargy, to force people to think, and especially to think about the conceptions with which they supposed themselves to be most familiar, those which guided their conduct in private and public affairs—justice, expediency, honesty, and the like—such was the constant object of his life. That he should have made enemies, that he should have been misunderstood, that he should have been accused of undermining the foundations of morality and religion, is natural and intelligible enough; and it was on these grounds that he was condemned to death. His conduct at his trial was of a piece with the rest of his life. The customary arts of the pleader, the appeal to the sympathies of the public, the introduction into court of weeping wife and children, he rejected as unworthy of himself and of his cause.

[1] Plato, Lysis 206 e.—Translated by Jowett.

His defence was a simple exposition of the character and the aims of his life; so far from being a criminal he asserted that he was a benefactor of the Athenian people; and having, after his condemnation, to suggest the sentence he thought appropriate, he proposed that he should be supported at the public expense as one who had deserved well of his country. After his sentence to death, having to wait thirty days for its execution, he showed no change from his customary cheerfulness, passing his time in conversation with his friends. So far from regretting his fate he rather congratulated himself that he would escape the decadence that attends upon old age; and he had, if we may trust Plato, a fair and confident assurance that a happy life awaited him beyond. He died, according to the merciful law of Athens, by drinking hemlock; "the wisest and justest and best," in Plato's judgment, "of all the men that I have ever known."

We have dwelt thus long on the personality of Socrates, familiar though it be, not only on account of its intrinsic interest, but also because it is peculiarly Hellenic. That sunny and frank intelligence, bathed, as it were, in the open air, a gracious blossom springing from the root of physical health, that unique and perfect balance of body and soul, passion and intellect, represent, against the brilliant setting of Athenian life, the highest achievement of the civilization of Greece. The figure of Socrates, no doubt, has been idealized by Plato, but it is none the less significant of the trend of Hellenic life. No other people could have conceived such an ideal; no other could have gone so far towards its realization.

§ 8. THE GREEK VIEW OF WOMAN

In the preceding account we have attempted to give some conception of the Greek ideal for the individual man. It is now time to remind ourselves that that ideal was only supposed to be proper to a small class—the class of soldier-citizens. Artisans and slaves, as we have seen, had no participation in it; neither, and that is our next point, had women.

Nothing more profoundly distinguishes the Hellenic from the modern view of life than the estimate in which women were held by the Greeks. Their opinion on this point was partly the cause and partly the effect of that preponderance of the idea of the state on which we have already dwelt, and from which it followed naturally enough that marriage should be regarded primarily as a means of producing healthy and efficient citizens. This view is best illustrated by the institutions of such a state as Sparta, where, as we saw, the woman was specially trained for maternity, and connections outside the marriage tie were sanctioned by custom and opinion, if they were such as were likely to lead to healthy offspring. Further it may be noted that in almost every state the exposure of deformed or sickly infants was encouraged by law, the child being thus regarded, from the beginning, as a member of the state, rather than as a member of the family.

The same view is reflected in the speculations of political philosophers. Plato, indeed, in his Republic, goes so far as to eliminate the family relation altogether. Not only is the whole connection between men and women to be regulated by the state, in respect both of the persons and of the limit of age within which they may associate, but the children as soon as they are born are to be carried off to a common nursery, there to be reared together, undistinguished by the mothers, who will suckle indifferently any infant that might happen to be assigned to them for the purpose. Here, as in other instances, Plato goes far beyond the limits set by the current sentiment of the Greeks, and in his later work is reluctantly constrained to abandon his scheme of community of wives and children. Yet even there he makes it compulsory on every man to marry between the ages of thirty and thirty-five, under penalty of fine and civil disabilities. Plato, no doubt, as we have said, exaggerates the opinions of his time; but the view, which he pushes to its extreme, of the subordination of the family to the state, was one, as we have already pointed out, which did predominate in Greece. It reappears in a soberer form in the treatise of Aristotle. He too would regulate by law both the age at which marriages should take place and the number of children that should be produced, and would have all deformed infants exposed. And here, no doubt, he is speaking in

conformity if not with the practice, at least with
the feeling of Greece. The modern conception
that the marriage relation is a matter of private
concern, and that any individual has a right to wed
whom and when he will, and to produce children
at his own discretion, regardless of all considerations of health and decency, was one altogether
alien to the Greeks. In theory at least, and to
some extent in practice (as for example in the case
of Sparta), they recognized that the production
of children was a business of supreme import to
the state, and that it was right and proper that it
should be regulated by law with a view to the
advantage of the whole community.

And if now we turn from considering the family
in its relation to the state to regard it in its relation to the individual, we are struck once more
by a divergence from the modern point of view,
or rather from the view which is supposed to prevail, particularly by writers of fiction, at any rate
in modern English life. In ancient Greece, so far
as our knowledge goes, there was little or no romance connected with the marriage tie. Marriage
was a means of producing legitimate children; that
is how it is defined by Demosthenes; and we have
no evidence that it was ever regarded as anything
more. In Athens we know that marriages were
commonly arranged by the father, much as they
are in modern France, on grounds of age, property,
connection and the like, and without any regard
for the inclination of the parties concerned. And

an interesting passage in Xenophon indicates a point of view quite consonant with this accepted practice. God, he says, ordained the institution of marriage; but on what grounds? Not in the least for the sake of the personal relation that might be established between the husband and wife, but for ends quite external and indifferent to any affection that might exist between them. First, for the perpetuation of the human race; secondly, to raise up protectors for the father in his old age; thirdly, to secure an appropriate division of labour, the man performing the outdoor work, the women guarding and superintending at home, and each thus fulfilling duly the function for which they were designed by nature. This eminently prosaic way of conceiving the marriage relation is also, it would seem, eminently Greek; and it leads us to consider more particularly the opinion prevalent in Greece of the nature and duty of women in general.

Here the first point to be noticed is the wide difference of the view represented in the Homeric poems from that which meets us in the historic period. Readers of the Iliad and the Odyssey will find depicted there, amid all the barbarity of an age of rapine and war, relations between men and women so tender, faithful and beautiful, that they may almost stand as universal types of the ultimate human ideal. Such for example is the relation between Odysseus and Penelope, the wife waiting year by year for the husband whose fate is unknown, wooed in vain by suitors who waste her substance and wear her life, nightly "watering her

bed with her tears" for twenty weary years, till
at last the wanderer returns, and "at once her knees
were loosened and her heart melted within her . . .
and she fell a weeping and ran straight towards him,
and cast her hands about his neck, and kissed his
head;" for "even as the sight of the land is welcome
to mariners, so welcome to her was the sight of her
lord, and her white arms would never quite leave
hold of his neck." [1]

Such, again, is the relation between Hector and
Andromache as described in the well-known scene
of the Iliad, where the wife comes out with her
babe to take leave of the husband on his way to
battle. "It were better for me," she cries, "to go
down to the grave if I lose thee; for never will any
comfort be mine when once thou, even thou, hast
met thy fate, but only sorrow. . . . Thou art to
me father and lady mother, yea, and brother, even
as thou art my goodly husband. Come now, have
pity and abide here upon the tower, lest thou make
thy child an orphan and thy wife a widow." Hector
answers with the plea of honour. He cannot draw
back, but he foresees defeat; and in his anticipation
of the future nothing is so bitter as the fate he fears
for his wife. "Yet doth the conquest of the
Trojans hereafter not so much trouble me, neither
Hekabe's own, neither King Priam's, neither my
brethren's, the many and brave that shall fall in
the dust before their foemen, as doth thine anguish
in the day when some mail-clad Achaian shall lead

[1] Odyss. XXIII. 205, 231.—Translated by Butcher and
Lang.

thee weeping and rob thee of the light of freedom.
. . . But me in death may the heaped-up earth be
covering, ere I hear thy crying and thy carrying
into captivity." [1]

But most striking of all the portraits of women
to be found in Homer, and most typical of a frank
and healthy relation between the sexes, is the
account of Nausicaa given in the Odyssey. Ulysses,
shipwrecked and naked, battered and covered with
brine, surprises Nausicaa and her maidens as they
are playing at ball on the shore. The attendants
run away, but Nausicaa remains to hear what the
stranger has to say. He asks her for shelter and
clothing; and she grants the request, with an exquisite courtesy and a freedom from all embarrass-
ment which becomes only the more marked and the
more delightful when, as she sees him emerge from
the bath, clothed and beautiful, she cannot restrain
the exclamation "would that such a one might be
called my husband, dwelling here, and that it may
please him here to abide." [2] About the whole scene
there is a freshness and a fragrance as of early
morning, and a tone so natural, free and frank,
that in the face of this rustic idyl the later centuries
sicken and faint, like candle-light in the splendour
of the dawn.

If we had only Homer to give us our ideas of
the Greeks, we might conclude, from such passages
as these, that they had a conception of woman
and of her relation to man, finer and nobler in some

---

[1] Iliad VI. 450.—Translated by Lang, Leaf and Myers.
[2] Od. VI. 244.—Translated by Butcher and Lang.

respects, than that of modern times. But in fact
the Homeric poems represent a civilization which
had passed away before the opening of the period
with which at present we are chiefly concerned.
And in the interval, for reasons which we need not
here attempt to state, a change had taken place
in the whole way of regarding the female sex.
So far, at any rate, as our authorities enable us to
judge, woman in the historic age was conceived
to be so inferior to man that he recognized in her
no other end than to minister to his pleasure or to
become the mother of his children. Romance and
the higher championship of intellect and spirit do
not appear (with certain notable exceptions) to
have been commonly sought or found in this relation. Woman, in fact, was regarded as a means,
not as an end; and was treated in a manner consonant with this view. Of this estimate many illustra-
tions might be adduced from the writers of the fifth
and fourth centuries. Plato, for example, classes
together "children, women, and servants," [1] and
states generally that there is no branch of human industry in which the female sex is not inferior to
the male.[2] Similarly, Aristotle insists again and
again on the natural inferiority of woman, and
illustrates it by such quaint observations as the
following: "A man would be considered a coward
who was only as brave as a brave woman, and a
woman as a chatterbox who was only as modest as
a good man." [3] But the most striking example,

[1] Plato, Republic 431 c.   [2] Ibid. 455 c.
[3] Arist. Pol. III. 1277 b 21.—Translated by Welldon.

perhaps, because the most unconscious, of this habitual way of regarding women is to be found in the funeral oration put by Thucydides into the mouth of Pericles, where the speaker, after suggesting what consolation he can to the fathers of the slain, turns to the women with the brief but significant exhortation: "If I am to speak of womanly virtues to those of you who will henceforth be widows, let me sum them up in one short admonition: To a woman not to show more weakness than is natural to her sex is a great glory, and not to be talked about for good or for evil among men." [1]

The sentiments of the poets are less admissible as evidence; but some of them are so extreme that they may be adduced as a further indication of a point of view whose prevalence alone could render them even dramatically plausible. Such for example is the remark of one of the characters in "Menander," "a woman is necessarily an evil, and he is a lucky man who catches her in the mildest form." While the general Greek view of the dependence of woman on man is well expressed in the words of Aethra, in the "Suppliants" of Euripides: "It is proper for women who are wise to let men act for them in everything." [2]

In accordance with this conception of the inferiority of the female sex, and partly as a cause, partly as an effect of it, we find that the position of the wife in ancient Greece was simply that of the domestic drudge. To stay at home and mind the

[1] Thucydides II. 45.—Translated by Jowett.
[2] Euripides, Hik. 40.

house was her recognized ideal. "A free woman should be bounded by the street door," says one of the characters in Menander; and another writer discriminates as follows the functions of the two sexes: "War, politics, and public speaking are the sphere of man; that of woman is to keep house, to stay at home and to receive and tend her husband." We are not surprised, therefore, to find that the symbol of woman is the tortoise; and in the following burlesque passage from Aristophanes we shall recognize, in spite of the touch of caricature, the genuine features of the Greek wife. Praxagora is recounting the merits and services of women:

"They dip their wool in hot water according to the ancient plan, all of them without exception, and never make the slightest innovation. They sit and cook, as of old. They carry upon their heads, as of old. They conduct the Themophoriae, as of old. They wear out their husbands, as of old. They buy sweets, as of old." [1]

And that this was also the kind of ideal approved by their lords and masters, and that any attempt to pass beyond it was resented, is amusingly illustrated in the following extract from the same poet, where Lysistrata explains the growing indignation of the women at the bad conduct of affairs by the men, and the way in which their attempts to interfere were resented. The comments of the "magistrate" typify, of course, the man's point of view.

[1] Aristophanes, Eccles. 215.

"Think of our old moderation and gentleness, think how
　　we bore with your pranks, and were still,
All through the days of your former prognacity, all
　　through the war that is over and spent:
Not that (be sure) we approved of your policy; never our
　　griefs you allowed us to vent.
Well we perceived your mistakes and mismanagement.
　　Often at home on our housekeeping cares,
Often we heard of some foolish proposal you made for
　　conducting the public affairs.
Then would we question you mildly and pleasantly,
　　inwardly grieving, but outwardly gay;
'Husband, how goes it abroad?' we would ask of him;
　　what have ye done in Assembly to-day?'
'What would ye write on the side of the Treaty-stone?'
　　Husband says angrily, 'What's that to you?
You hold your tongue!'　And I held it accordingly.

STRATYLLIS.

That is a thing which I never would do!

MAGISTRATE.

Ma'am, if you hadn't you'd soon have repented it.

LYSISTRATA.

Therefore I held it, and spake not a word.
Soon of another tremendous absurdity, wilder and worse
　　than the former, we heard.
'Husband,' I say, with a tender solicitude, 'why have you
　　passed such a foolish decree?'
Viciously, moodily, glaring askance at me, 'Stick to your
　　spinning, my mistress,' says he,
'Else you will speedily find it the worse for you! war is
　　the care and business of men!'

MAGISTRATE.
Zeus! 'twas a worthy reply, and an excellent!

LYSISTRATA.
What! you unfortunate, shall we not then,
Then, when we see you perplexed and incompetent, shall
    we not tender advice to the state!" [1]

The conception thus indicated in burlesque of
the proper place of woman is expressed more
seriously, from the point of view of the average
man, in the "Oeconomicus" of Xenophon. Ischomachus, the hero of that work, with whom we have
already made acquaintance, gives an account of his
own wife, and of the way in which he had trained
her. When he married her, he explains, she was
not yet fifteen, and had been brought up with the
utmost care "that she might see, hear, and ask as
little as possible." Her accomplishments were
weaving and a sufficient acquaintance with all that
concerns the stomach; and her attitude towards her
husband she expressed in the single phrase:
"Everything rests with you; my duty, my mother
said, is simply to be modest." Ischomachus pro-
ceeds to explain to her the place he expects her to
fill; she is to suckle his children, to cook, and to
superintend the house; and for this purpose God has
given her special gifts, different from but not
necessarily inferior to those of man. Husband and
wife naturally supply one another's deficiencies;
and if the wife perform her function worthily she

[1] Aristoph. Lysistrata. 507.—Translated by B. B.
Rogers.

may even make herself the ruling partner, and be sure that as she grows older she will be held not less but more in honour, as the guardian of her children and the stewardess of her husband's goods. —In Xenophon's view, in fact, the inferiority of the woman almost disappears; and the sentiment approximates closely to that of Tennyson—

> "either sex alone
> Is half itself, and in true marriage lies
> Nor equal, nor unequal: each fulfils
> Defect in each."

Such a conception, however, of the "complementary" relation of woman to man, does not exclude a conviction of her essential inferiority. And this conviction, it can hardly be disputed, was a cardinal point in the Greek view of life.

§ 9. Protests against the Common View of Woman

Nevertheless, there are not wanting indications, both in theory and practice, of a protest against it. In Sparta, as we have already noticed, girls, instead of being confined to the house, were brought up in the open air among the boys, trained in gymnastics and accustomed to run and wrestle naked. And Plato, modelling his view upon this experience, makes no distinction of the sexes in his ideal republic. Women, he admits, are generally inferior to men, but they have similar, if lower, capacities and powers. There is no occupation or art for which they may not be fitted by nature and education; and he would therefore have them take their share in government and war, as well as in the various mechanical trades. "None of the occupations," he says, "which comprehend the ordering of a state, belong to woman as woman, nor yet to man as man; but natural gifts are to be found here and there, in both sexes alike; and, so far as her nature is concerned, the woman is admissible to all pursuits as well as the man; though in all of them the woman is weaker than the man." [1]

In adopting this attitude Plato stands alone not only among the Greeks, but one might almost say, among mankind, till we come to the latest views of the nineteenth century. But there is another Greek, the poet Euripides, who, without advancing any theory about the proper position of women, yet displays so intimate an understanding of their difficulties, and so warm and close a sympathy with their griefs, that some of his utterances may stand to all time as documents of the dumb and age-long protest of the weaker against the stronger sex. In illustration we may cite the following lines from the "Medea," applicable, *mutatis mutandis,* to how many generations of suffering wives?

"Of all things that have life and sense we women are most wretched. For we are compelled to buy with gold a husband who is also—worst of all!—the master of our person. And on his character, good or bad, our whole fate depends. For divorce is

[1] Plato, Rep. 455 d.—Translated by Davies and Vaughan.

regarded as a disgrace to a woman and she cannot repudiate her husband. Then coming as she does into the midst of manners and customs strange to her, she would need the gift of divination—unless she has been taught at home—to know how best to treat her bed-fellow. And if we manage so well that our husband remains faithful to us, and does not break away, we may think ourselves fortunate; if not, there is nothing for it but death. A man when he is vexed at home can go out and find relief among his friends or acquaintances; but we women have none to look to but him. They tell us we live a sheltered life at home while they go to the wars; but that is nonsense. For I would rather go into battle thrice than bear a child once." [1]

Hitherto we have been speaking mainly of the position of the wife in Greece. It is necessary now to say a few words about that class of women who were called in the Greek tongue Hetæræ; and who are by some supposed to have represented, intellectually at least, a higher level of culture than the other members of their sex. In exceptional cases, this, no doubt, was the fact. Aspasia, for example, the mistress of Pericles, was famous for her powers of mind. According to Plato she was an accomplished rhetorician, and the real composer of the celebrated funeral oration of Pericles; and Plutarch asserts that she was courted and admired by the statesmen and philosophers of Greece. But Aspasia cannot be taken as a type of the Hetæræ of Greece. That these women, by the variety and

[1] Euripides, Med. 230.

freedom of their life, may and must have acquired
certain qualities of character and mind that could
hardly be developed in the seclusion of the Greek
home, may readily be admitted; we know, for example, that they cultivated music and the power
of conversation; and were welcome guests at supper-
parties. But we have no evidence that the relations which they formed rested as a rule on any
but the simplest physical basis. The real distinction, under this head, between the Greek point
of view and our own, appears to lie rather in the
frankness with which this whole class of relations
was recognized by the Greeks. There were temples
in honour of Aphrodite Pandemos, the goddess of
illicit love, and festivals celebrated in her honour;
statues were erected of famous courtesans, of
Phryne for example, at Delphi, between two kings;
and philosophers and statesmen lived with their
mistresses openly, without any loss of public reputation. Every man, said the orator Demosthenes,
requires besides his wife at least two mistresses;
and this statement, made as a matter of course in
open court, is perhaps the most curious illustration
we possess of the distinction between the Greek
civilization and our own, as regards not the fact
itself but the light in which it was viewed.

§ 10. FRIENDSHIP

From what has been said about the Greek view
of women, it might naturally have been supposed
that there can have been little place in their life for

all that we designate under the term "romance."
Personal affection, as we have seen, was not the
basis of married life; and relations with Hetæræ
appear to have been, in this respect, no finer or
higher than similar relations in our own times.
Nevertheless, it would be a mistake to conclude,
from these conditions, that the element of romance
was absent from Greek life. The fact is simply that
with them it took a different form, that of passionate
friendship between men. Such friendships, of
course, occur in all nations and at all times, but
among the Greeks, they were, we might say, an
institution. Their ideal was the development and
education of the younger by the older man, and in
this view they were recognized and approved by
custom and law as an important factor in the state.
In Sparta, for example, it was the rule that every
boy had attached to him some elder youth by
whom he was constantly attended, admonished, and
trained, and who shared in public estimation the
praise and blame of his acts; so that it is even reported that on one occasion a Spartan boy having
cried out in a fight, not he himself but his friend
was fined for the lapse of self-control. The custom
of Sparta existed also in Crete. But the most remarkable instance of the deliberate dedication of
this passion to political and military ends is that
of the celebrated "Theban band," a troop consist-
ing exclusively of pairs of lovers, who marched and
fought in battle side by side, and by their presence
and example inspired one another to a courage so
constant and high that "it is stated that they were

never beaten till the battle at Chæronea: and when
Philip, after the fight, took a view of the slain,
and came to the place where the three hundred that
fought his phalanx lay dead together, he wondered,
and understanding that it was the band of lovers,
he shed tears, and said, "Perish any man who
suspects that these men either did or suffered anything that was base." [1]

Greek legend and history, in fact resounds with
the praises of friends. Achilles and Patroclus,
Pylades and Orestes, Harmodius and Aristogeiton,
Solon and Peisistratus, Socrates and Alcibiades,
Epaminondas and Pelopidas,—these are names that
recall at once all that is highest in the achievement
and all that is most romantic in the passion of
Greece. For it was the prerogative of this form of
love, in its finer manifestations, that it passed
beyond persons to objective ends, linking emotion
to action in a life of common danger and toil. Not
only, nor primarily, the physical sense was touched,
but mainly and in chief the imagination and intellect. The affection of Achilles for Patroclus is as
intense as that of a lover for his mistress, but it has
in addition a body and depth such as only years
of common labour could impart. "Achilles wept,
remembering his dear comrade, nor did sleep that
conquereth all take hold of him, but he kept turning himself to this side and to that, yearning for
Patroclus' manhood and excellent valour, and all the
toils he achieved with him and the woes he bare,

[1] Plutarch, Pelopidas. ch. 18—Ed. by Clough.

cleaving the battles of men and the grievous waves.
As he thought thereon he shed big tears, now lying
on his side, now on his back, now on his face; and
then anon he would arise upon his feet and roam
wildly beside the beach of the salt sea." [1]   That is
the ideal spirit of Greek comradeship—each sup-
porting the other in his best efforts and aims, mind
assisting mind and hand hand, and the end of the
love residing not in an easy satisfaction of itself, but
in the development and perfecting of the souls in
which it dwelt.

Of such a love we have a record in the elegies of
Theognis, in which the poet has embodied, for the
benefit of Kurnus his friend, the ripe experience of
an eventful life.   The poems for the most part are
didactic in character, consciously and deliberately
aimed at the instruction and guidance of the man
to whom they are addressed; but every now and
again the passion breaks through which informs and
inspires this virile intercourse, and in such a passage
as the following gives us the key to this and to all
the finer friendships of the Greeks:

"Lo, I have given thee wings wherewith to fly
    Over the boundless ocean and the earth;
Yea, on the lips of many shalt thou lie,
    The comrade of their banquet and their mirth.
Youths in their loveliness shall bid thee sound
    Upon the silver flute's melodious breath;
And when thou goest darkling underground
    Down to the lamentable house of death,

[1] Iliad XXIV. 3.—Translated by Lang, Leaf, and
Myers.

Oh yet not then from honour shalt thou cease
   But wander, an imperishable name,
Kurnus, about the seas and shores of Greece,
Crossing from isle to isle the barren main.
Horses thou shalt not need, but lightly ride
   Sped by the Muses of the violet crown,
And men to come, while earth and sun abide,
   Who cherish song shall cherish thy renown.
Yea, I have given thee wings, and in return
   Thou givest me the scorn with which I burn." [1]

It was his insistence on friendship as an incentive
to a noble life that was the secret of the power
of Socrates. Listen, for example, to the account
which Plutarch gives of his influence upon the
young Alcibiades:

"Alcibiades, listening now to language entirely
free from every thought of unmanly fondness and
silly displays of affection, finding himself with one
who sought to lay open to him the deficiencies of
his mind, and repress his vain and foolish arrogance,

   'Dropped like the craven cock his conquered wing.'

He esteemed these endeavours of Socrates as most
truly a means which the gods made use of for the
care and preservation of youth, and began to think
meanly of himself, and to admire him; to be pleased
with his kindness, and to stand in awe of his virtue;
and, unawares to himself, there became formed in
his mind that reflex image and reciprocation of love,
or Anteros, that Plato talks of. . . . Though Socrates had many and powerful rivals, yet the natural

   [1] Theognis, 237.

good qualities of Alcibiades gave his affection the mastery. His words overcame him so much, as to draw tears from his eyes, and to disturb his very soul. Yet sometimes he would abandon himself to flatterers, when they proposed to him varieties of pleasure, and would desert Socrates; who then would pursue him, as if he had been a fugitive slave. He despised every one else, and had no reverence or awe for any but him." [1]

The relation thus established may be further illustrated by the following graceful little anecdote. Socrates and Alcibiades were fellow-soldiers at Potidæa and shared the same tent. In a stiff engagement both behaved with gallantry. At last Alcibiades fell wounded, and Socrates, standing over him, defended and finally saved him. For this he might fairly have claimed the customary prize of valour; but he insisted on resigning it to his friend, as an incentive to his "ambition for noble deeds."

Another illustration of the power of this passion to evoke and stimulate courage is given in the story of Cleomachus, narrated by Plutarch. In a battle between the Chalcidians and the Eretrians, the cavalry of the former being hard pressed, Cleomachus was called upon to make a diversion. He turned to his friend and asked him if he intended to be a spectator of the struggle; the youth replied in the affirmative, and embracing his friend, with his own hands buckled on his helmet; whereupon Cleomachus charged with impetuosity, routed the foe and died gloriously fighting. And thence-

[1] Plut. Alc. ch. 4.—Ed. by Clough.

forth, says Plutarch, the Chalcidians, who had
previously mistrusted such friendships, cultivated
and honoured them more than any other people.

So much indeed were the Greeks impressed with
the manliness of this passion, with its power to
prompt to high thought and heroic action, that some
of the best of them set the love of man for man far
above that of man for woman.   The one, they maintained, was primarily of the spirit, the other primarily of the flesh; the one bent upon shaping to the
type of all manly excellence both the body and the
soul of the beloved, the other upon a passing
pleasure of the senses.   And they noted that among
the barbarians, who were subject to tyrants, this
passion was discouraged, along with gymnastics and
philosophy, because it was felt by their masters that
it would be fatal to their power; so essentially was
it the prerogative of freedom, so incompatible with
the nature and the status of a slave.

It is in the works of Plato that this view is most
completely and exquisitely set forth.   To him, love
is the beginning of all wisdom; and among all the
forms of love, that one in chief, which is conceived
by one man for another, of which the main operation
and end is in the spirit, and which leads on and out
from the passion for a particular body and soul to an
enthusiasm for that highest beauty, wisdom, and
excellence, of which the most perfect mortal forms
are but a faint and inadequate reflection.   Such a
love is the initiation into the higher life, the spring
at once of virtue, of philosophy, and of religion.
Always operative in practice in Greek life it was not

invented but interpreted by Plato. The philosopher merely gave an ideal expression to what was stirring in the heart of every generous youth; and the passage which we have selected for quotation may be taken as representative not only of the personality of Plato, but of the higher aspect of a characteristic phase of Greek civilization.

"And now, taking my leave of you, I will rehearse a tale of love which I heard from Diotima of Mantineia, a woman wise in this and in many other kinds of knowledge. She was my instructress in the art of love, and I shall repeat to you what she said to me: 'On the birthday of Aphrodite there was a feast of the gods, at which the god Poros or Plenty, who is the son of Metis or Discretion, was one of the guests. When the feast was over, Penia or Poverty, as the manner is on such occasions, came about the doors to beg. Now Plenty, who was the worse for nectar (there was no wine in those days), went into the garden of Zeus and fell into a heavy sleep; and Poverty considering her own straitened circumstances, plotted to have a child by him, and accordingly she lay down at his side and conceived Love, who partly because he is naturally a lover of the beautiful, and because Aphrodite is herself beautiful, and also because he was born on her birthday, is her follower and attendant. And as his parentage is, so also are his fortunes. In the first place he is always poor, and anything but tender and fair, as the many imagine him; and he is rough and squalid, and has no shoes, nor a house to dwell in; on the bare earth exposed he lies under the open heaven, in the streets, or at the doors of houses, taking his rest; and like his mother he is always in distress. Like his father too, whom he also partly resembles, he is always plotting against the fair and good; he is bold, enterprising, strong, a mighty hunter, always weaving some intrigue or other, keen in the pursuit of wisdom, fertile in resources; a philosopher at all times, terrible as an enchanter, sorcerer, sophist. He is by nature neither mortal nor immortal, but alive and flourishing at one moment when he is in plenty, and dead at another moment, and again alive by reason of his father's nature. But that which is always flowing in is always flowing out, and so he is never in want and never in wealth; and, further, he is in a mean between ignorance and knowledge. The truth of the matter is this: No god is a philosopher or seeker after wisdom, neither do the ignorant seek after wisdom. For herein is the evil of ignorance, that he who is neither good nor wise is nevertheless satisfied with himself: he has no desire for that of which he feels no want.' 'But who then, Diotima,' I said, 'are the lovers of wisdom, if they are neither the wise nor the foolish?' 'A child may answer that question,' she replied; 'they are those who are in a mean between the two: Love is one of them. For wisdom is a most beautiful thing, and Love is of the beautiful; and therefore Love is also a philosopher or lover of wisdom, and being a lover of wisdom is in a mean between the wise and the ignorant. And of this too his birth is the cause; for his father is wealthy and wise, and his mother poor and foolish.

Such, my dear Socrates, is the nature of the spirit Love.'

"I said: 'O thou stranger woman, thou sayest well; but, assuming Love to be such as you say, what is the use of him to man?'

" 'That, Socrates,' she replied, 'I will attempt to unfold: of his nature and birth I have already spoken; and you acknowledge that Love is of the beautiful. But some one will say: Of the beautiful in what, Socrates and Diotima? or rather let me put the question more clearly, and ask: When a man loves the beautiful, what does he desire?'

"I answered her, 'That the beautiful may be his.'

" 'Still,' she said, 'the answer suggests a further question: What is given by the possession of beauty?'

" 'To what you have asked,' I said, 'I have no answer ready.'

" 'Then,' she said, 'let me put the word "good" in the place of "beautiful," and repeat the question once more: If he who loves, loves the good, what is it then that he loves?'

" 'The possession of the good,' I said.

" 'And what does he gain who possesses the good?'

" 'Happiness,' I replied; 'there is less difficulty in answering that question.'

" 'Yes,' she said, 'the happy are made happy by the acquisition of good things. Nor is there any need to ask why a man desires happiness; the answer is already final.'

" 'You are right,' I said.

" 'And is this wish and this desire common to all? and do all men always desire their own good, or only some men?—what say you?'

" 'All men,' I replied; 'the desire is common to all.'

" 'Then,' she said, 'the simple truth is that men love the good.'

" 'Yes,' I said.

" 'To which must be added that they love the possession of the good?'

" 'That must be added too.'

" 'Then love,' she said, 'may be described generally as the love of the everlasting possession of the good?'

" 'That is most true.'

" 'Then if this be the nature of love, can you tell me further,' she said, 'what is the manner of the pursuit? what are they doing who show all this eagerness and heat which is called love? and what is the object which they have in view? Answer me.'

" 'Nay, Diotima,' I replied, 'if I had known, I should not have wondered at your wisdom, neither should I have come to learn from you about this very matter.'

" 'Well,' she said, 'I will teach you:—The object which they have in view is birth in beauty, whether of body or soul.'

" 'I do not understand you,' I said; 'the oracle requires an explanation.'

" 'I will make my meaning clearer,' she replied. 'I mean to say, that all men are bringing to the birth in their bodies and in their souls. There is a certain age at which human nature is desirous of procreation—procreation which must be in beauty and not in deformity; and this procreation is the union of man and woman, and is a divine thing: for conception and generation are an immortal principle in the mortal creature, and in the inharmonious they can never be. But the deformed is always inharmonious with the divine, and the beautiful harmonious. Beauty, then, is the destiny or goddess of parturition who presides at birth, and therefore, when approaching beauty, the conceiving power is propitious, and diffusive, and benign, and begets and bears fruit: at the sight of ugliness she frowns and contracts and has a sense of pain, and turns away, and shrivels up, and not without a pang refrains from conception. And this is the reason why, when the hour of conception arrives, and the teeming nature is full, there is such a flutter and ecstasy about beauty whose approach is the alleviation of the pain of travail. For love, Socrates, is not as you imagine, the love of the beautiful only:'

" 'What then?'

" 'The love of generation and of birth in beauty.'

" 'Yes,' I said.

" 'Yes indeed,' she replied.

" 'But why of generation?'

" 'Because to the mortal creature, generation is a sort of eternity and immortality,' she replied; 'and if, as has been already admitted, love is of the everlasting possession of the good, all men will necessarily desire immortality together with good: wherefore love is of immortality.'

"I was astonished at her words and said: 'Is this really true, O thou wise Diotima?'

"And she answered with all the authority of an accomplished sophist: 'Of that, Socrates, you may be assured;—think only of the ambition of men, and you will wonder at the senselessness of their ways, unless you consider how they are stirred by the love of an immortality of fame. They are ready to run all risks greater far then they would have run for their children, and to spend money and undergo any sort of toil, and even to die, for the sake of leaving behind them a name which shall be eternal. Do you imagine that Alcestis would have died to save Admetus, or Achilles to avenge Patroclus, or your own Codrus in order to preserve the kingdom for his sons, if they had not imagined that the memory of their virtues, which still survives among us, would be immortal? Nay,' she said, 'I am persuaded that all men do all things, and the better they are the more they do them, in hope of the glorious fame of immortal virtue; for they desire the immortal.

" 'Those who are pregnant in the body only, betake themselves to women and beget children— this is the character of their love: their offspring, as they hope, will preserve their memory and give them the blessedness and immortality which they desire in the future. But souls which are pregnant—for there certainly are men who are more creative in their souls than in their bodies—conceive that which is proper for the soul to conceive or contain. And what are these conceptions? wisdom and virtue in general. And such creators are poets and all artists who are deserving of the name inventor. But the greatest and fairest sort of wisdom by far is that which is concerned with the ordering of states and families, and which is called temperance and justice. And he who in youth has the seed of these implanted in him and is himself inspired, when he comes to maturity desires to beget and generate. He wanders about, seeking beauty that he may beget offspring—for in deformity he will beget nothing—and naturally embraces the beautiful rather than the deformed body; above all, when he finds a fair and noble and well-nurtured soul, he embraces the two in one person, and to such a one he is full of speech about virtue and the nature and pursuits of a good man; and he tries to educate him; and at the touch of the beautiful which is ever present to his memory, even when absent, he brings forth that which he had conceived long before, and in company with him tends that which he brings forth; and they are married by a far nearer tie and have a closer friendship than those who beget mortal children, for the children who are their common offspring are fairer and more immortal. Who, when he thinks of Homer and Hesiod and other great poets, would not rather have their children than ordinary ones? Who would not emulate them in the creation of children such as theirs, which have preserved their memory and given them everlasting glory? Or who would not have such children as Lycurgus left behind him to be the saviours not only of Lacedæmon, but of Hellas, as one may say? There is Solon, too, who is the revered father of

Athenian laws; and many others there are in many
other places, both among Hellenes and barbarians,
who have given to the world many noble works,
and have been the parents of virtue of every kind;
and many temples have been raised in their honour
for the sake of children such as theirs; which were
never raised in honour of any one, for the sake of
his mortal children.

" 'These are the lesser mysteries of love, into
which even you, Socrates, may enter; to the greater
and more hidden ones which are the crown of these,
and to which, if you pursue them in a right spirit,
they will lead, I know not whether you will be able
to attain.   But I will do my utmost to inform you,
and do you follow if you can.   For he who would
proceed aright in this matter should begin in youth
to visit beautiful forms; and first, if he be guided by
his instructor aright, to love one such form only—
out of that he should create fair thoughts; and soon
he will of himself perceive that the beauty of one
form is akin to the beauty of another; and then if
beauty of form in general is his pursuit, how foolish
would he be not to recognize that the beauty in every
form is one and the same!   And when he perceives
this he will abate his violent love of the one, which
he will despise and deem a small thing, and will
become a lover of all beautiful forms.   In the next
stage he will consider that the beauty of the mind
is more honourable than the outward form.   So
that, if a virtuous soul have but a little comeliness,
he will be content to love and tend him, and will
search out and bring to the birth thoughts which

may improve the young, until he is compelled to contemplate and see the beauty of institutions and laws, and to understand that the beauty of them all is of one family, and that personal beauty is a trifle; and after laws and institutions he will go on to the sciences, that he may see their beauty, being not like a servant in love with the beauty of one youth or man or institution, himself a slave mean and narrow-minded, but drawing towards and contemplating the vast sea of beauty, he will create many fair and noble thoughts and notions in boundless love of wisdom; until on that store he grows and waxes strong, and at last the vision is revealed to him of a single science which is the science of beauty everywhere. To this I will proceed; please to give me your very best attention:

" 'He who has been instructed thus far in the things of love, and who has learned to see the beautiful in due order and succession, when he comes toward the end will suddenly perceive a nature of wondrous beauty (and this, Socrates, is the final cause of all our former toils)—a nature which in the first place is everlasting, not growing and decaying, or waxing and waning; secondly, not fair in one point of view and foul in another, or at one time or in one relation or in one place fair, at another time or in another relation or at another place foul, as if fair to some and foul to others, or in the likeness of a face or hands or any other part of the bodily frame, or in any form of speech or knowledge, or existing in any other being, as for example, in an animal, or in heaven, or in earth, or in any other place; but beauty absolute, separate, simple, and everlasting, which without diminution and without increase, or any change, is imparted to the ever-growing and perishing beauties of all other things. He who, from these ascending under the influence of true love, begins to perceive that beauty, is not far from the end. And the true order of going, or being led by another, to the things of love, is to begin from the beauties of earth and mount upwards for the sake of that other beauty, using these as steps only, and from one going on to two, and from two to all fair forms, and from fair forms to fair practices, and from fair practices to fair notions, until from fair notions he arrives at the notion of absolute beauty, and at last knows what the essence of beauty is. 'This, my dear Socrates,' said the stranger of Mantineia, 'is that life above all others which man should live, in the contemplation of beauty absolute: a beauty which if you once beheld, you would see not to be after the measure of gold, and garments, and fair boys and youths, whose presence now entrances you; and you and many a one would be content to live seeing them only and conversing with them without meat or drink, if that were possible,—you only want to look at them and to be with them. But what if man had eyes to see the true beauty—the divine beauty, I mean, pure and clear and unalloyed, not clogged with the pollutions of mortality and all the colours and vanities of human life—thither looking, and holding converse with the true beauty simple and divine?

Remember how in that communion only, behold-
ing beauty with the eye of the mind, he will be
enabled to bring forth, not images of beauty, but
realities (for he has hold not of an image but of a
reality), and bringing forth and nourishing true
virtue to become the friend of God and be immortal, if mortal man may. Would that be an
ignoble life?'

"Such, Phaedrus—and I speak not only to you,
but to all of you—were the words of Diotima; and
I am persuaded of their truth. And being persuaded of them, I try to persuade others, that in
the attainment of this end human nature will not
easily find a helper better than Love. And therefore, also, I say that every man ought to honour
him as I myself honour him, and walk in his ways,
and exhort others to do the same, and praise the
power and spirit of Love according to the measure
of my ability now and ever." [1]

I have thought it worth while to quote this passage, in spite of its length, partly for the sake of
its own intrinsic beauty, partly because no account
of the Greek view of life could be complete which
did not insist upon the prominence in their civilization of the passion of friendship, and its capacity
of being turned to the noblest uses. That there
was another side to the matter goes without saying. This passion, like any other, has its depths,
as well as its heights; and the ideal of friendship
conceived by Plato was as remote, perhaps, from

[1] Plato, Symp. 201.—Translated by Jowett.

the experience of the average man, as Dante's presentation of the love between man and woman. Still, the fact remains that it was friendship of this kind that supplied to the Greek that element of romance which plays so large a part in modern life; and it is to this, and not to the relations between men and women, that we must look for the highest reaches of their emotional experience.

§ 11. SUMMARY

If now we turn back to take a general view of the points that have been treated in the present chapter, we shall notice, in the first place, that the ideal of the Greeks was the direct and natural outcome of the conditions of their life. It was not something beyond and above the experience of the class to which it applied, but rather, was the formula of that experience itself: in philosophical phrase, it was immanent not transcendent. Because there really was a class of soldier-citizens free from the necessity of mechanical toil, possessed of competence and leisure, and devoting these advantages willingly to the service of the state, therefore their ideal of conduct took the form we have described. It was the ideal of a privileged class, and postulated for its realization, not only a strenuous endeavour on the part of the individual, but also certain adventitious gifts of fortune, such as health, wealth, and family connections. These were conditions that actually obtained among members of the class concerned; so that the ideal in question was not a mere abstract "ought," but an expression of what, approximately at least, was realized in fact.

But this, which was the strength of the ideal of the Greeks, was also its limitation. Their ethical system rested not only on universal facts of human nature, but also on a particular and transitory social arrangement. When therefore the city-state, with its sharp antithesis of classes, began to decline, the ideal of the soldier-citizen declined also. The conditions of its realization no longer existed, and ethical conceptions passed into a new phase. In the first place the ideal of conduct was extended so as to apply to man as man, instead of to a particular class in a particular form of state; and in the second place, as a corollary of this, those external goods of fortune which were the privilege of the few, could no longer be assumed as conditions of an ideal which was supposed to apply to all. Consequently, the new ideal was conceived as wholly internal. To be virtuous was to act under the control of the universal reason which was supposed to dwell in man as man; and such action was independent of all the gifts of chance. It was as open to a slave as to a freeman, to an artisan as to a soldier or a statesman. The changes and chances of this mortal life were indifferent to the virtuous man; on the rack as on the throne he was lord of himself and free.

This conception of the Stoics broke down the limitation of the Greek ideal by extending the possibility of virtue to all mankind. But at the same time it destroyed its sanity and balance. For it was precisely because of its limitation that the ideal of the Greeks was, approximately at least, an account of what was, and not merely of what ought to be. A man possessed of wealth and friends, of leisure, health, and culture, really could and did achieve the end at which he was aiming; but the conception of one who without any such advantages, on the contrary with positive disadvantages, poor, sickly, and a slave perhaps, or even in prison or on the rack, should nevertheless retain unimpaired the dignity of manhood and the freedom of his own soul,—such a conception if it is not chimerical, is at any rate so remote from common experience, that it is not capable of serving as a really practical ideal for ordinary life. But an ideal so remote that its realization is despaired of, is as good as none. And the conception of the Stoics, if it was more comprehensive than that of Aristotle, was also less practical and real.

By virtue, nevertheless, of this comprehensiveness, the Stoic ideal is more akin to modern tendencies than that of the soldier-citizen in the city-state. To provide for the excellence of a privileged class at the expense of the rest of the community is becoming to us increasingly impossible in fact and intolerable in idea. But while admitting this, we cannot but note that the Greeks, at whatever cost, did actually achieve a development of the individual more high and more complete than has been even approached by any other age. Whether it will ever be possible, under totally different conditions, to realize once more that balance of body and soul, that sanity of ethical intuition, that frank recognition of the whole range of our complex human nature with a view to its harmonious organization under the control of a lucid reason—whether it will ever be possible again to realize this ideal, and that not only in the members of a privileged class, but in the whole body of the state, is a question too problematical to be raised with advantage in this place. But it is impossible not to perceive that with the decline of the Greek city-state something passed from the world which it can never cease to regret, and the recovery of which, if it might be, in some more perfect form, must be the goal of its highest practical endeavours. Immense, no doubt, is the significance of the centuries that have intervened, but it is a significance of preparation; and when we look beyond the means to the wished-for end, limiting our conceptions to the actual possibilities of life on earth, it is among the Greeks that we seek the record of the highest achievement of the past. and the hope of the highest possibilities of the future.

CHAPTER IV

THE GREEK VIEW OF ART

§ 1. Greek Art an Expression of National Life

IN approaching the subject of the Art of the
Greeks we come to what, more plausibly than
any other, may be regarded as the central point
of their scheme of life. We have already noticed,
in dealing with other topics, how constantly the
æsthetic point of view emerges and predominates
in matters with which, in the modern way of looking at things, it appears to have no direct and
natural connection. We saw, for example, how inseparable in their religion was the element of ritual
and ceremony from that of idea; how in their
ethical conceptions the primary notion was that
of beauty; how they aimed throughout at a perfect balance of body and soul, and more generally,
in every department, at an expression of the inner
by the outer so complete and perfect that the conception of a separation of the two became almost
as impossible to their thought as it would have
been unpleasing and discordant to their feeling.
Now such a point of view is, in fact, that of art;
and philosophers of history have been amply justi-

fied in characterizing the whole Greek epoch as pre-eminently that of Beauty.

But if this be a true way of regarding the matter, we should expect to find that art and beauty had, for the Greeks, a very wide and complex significance. There is a view of art, and it is one that appears to be prevalent in our own time, which sets it altogether outside the general trend of national life and ideas; which asserts that it has no connection with ethics, religion, politics, or any of the general conceptions which regulate action and thought; that its end is in itself, and is simply beauty; and that in beauty there is no distinction of high or low, no preference of one kind above another. Art thus conceived is, in the first place, purely subjective in character; the artist alone is the standard, and any phase or mood of his, however exceptional, personal and transitory, is competent to produce a work of art as satisfying and as great as one whose inspiration was drawn from a nation's life, reflecting its highest moments, and its most universal aspirations and ideals; so that, for example, a butterfly drawn by Mr. Whistler would rank as high, say, as the Parthenon. And in the second place, in this view of art, the subject is a matter of absolute indifference. The standards of ordinary life, ethical or other, do not apply; there is no better or worse, but only a more or less beautiful; and the representation of a music-hall stage or a public-house bar may be as great and perfect a work of art as the Venus of Milo or the Madonna of Raphael.

This theory, which arises naturally and perhaps inevitably in an age where national life has degenerated into materialism and squalor, and the artist feels himself a stranger in a world of Philistines, we need not here pause to examine and criticize. It has been mentioned merely to illustrate by contrast the Greek view, which was diametrically opposed to this, and valued art in proportion as it represented in perfect form the highest and most comprehensive aspects of the national ideal.

To say this, is not, of course, to say that the Greek conception of art was didactic; for the word didactic, when applied to art, has usually the implication that the excellence of the moral is the only point to be considered, and that if that is good the work itself must be good. This idea does indeed occur in Greek thought—we find it, for example, paradoxically enough, in so great an artist as Plato—but if it had been the one which really determined their production, there would have been no occasion to write this chapter, for there would have been no Greek art to write about. The truer account of the impulse that urged them to create is that given also by Plato in an earlier and more impassioned work, in which he describes it as a "madness of those who are possessed by the Muses; which enters into a delicate and virgin soul, and there inspiring frenzy, awakens lyrical and all other numbers; with these adorning the myriad actions of ancient heroes for the instruction of posterity. But he who having no touch of the Muses' madness in his soul, comes to the door and thinks that he will get into the temple by the help of art—he, I say, and his poetry are not admitted; the sane man is nowhere at all when he enters into rivalry with the madman." [1]

The presupposition, in fact, of all that can be said about the Greek view of art, is that primarily and to begin with they were, by nature, artists. Judged simply by the æsthetic standard, without any consideration of subject matter at all, or any reference to intellectual or ethical ideals, they created works of art more purely beautiful than those of any other age or people. Their mere household crockery, their common pots and pans, are cast in shapes exquisitely graceful, and painted in designs admirably drawn and composed; and the little clay figures they used as we do china ornaments put to shame some of the most ambitious efforts of modern sculpture. Who, for example, would not rather look at a Tanagra statuette than at the equestrian statue of the Duke of Wellington?

The Greeks, in fact, quite apart from any theories they may have held, were artists through and through; and that is a fact we must carry with us through the whole of our discussion.

§ 2. IDENTIFICATION OF THE ÆSTHETIC AND ETHICAL POINTS OF VIEW

But on the other hand, it seems to be clear from all that we can learn, that their habitual way

[1] Plato, Phaedrus, 245 a.—Translated by Jowett.

of regarding works of art was not to judge them
simply and exclusively by their æsthetic value.
On the contrary, in criticizing two works otherwise equally beautiful, they would give a higher
place to the one or the other for its ethical or quasi-
ethical qualities. This indeed is what we should
expect from the comprehensive sense which, as we
have seen, attached in their tongue to the word
which we render "beautiful."

The æsthetic and ethical spheres, in fact, were
never sharply distinguished by the Greeks, and it
follows that as, on the one hand, their conception
of the good was identified with that of the beautiful, so, on the other hand, their conception of the
beautiful was identified with that of the good. Thus
the most beautiful work of art, in the Greek sense
of the term, was that which made the finest and
most harmonious appeal not only to the physical but
to the moral sense, and while communicating the
highest and most perfect pleasure to the eye or the
ear, had also the power to touch and inform the
soul with the grace which was her moral excellence.
Of this really characteristic Greek conception, this
fusion, so instinctive as to be almost unconscious,
of the æsthetic and ethical points of view, no better
illustration could be given than the following passage from the Republic of Plato, where the philosopher is describing the effect of beautiful works of
art, and especially of music, on the moral and intellectual character of his imaginary citizens:

  " 'We would not have our guardians grow up amid
images of moral deformity, as in some noxious

pasture, and there browse and feed upon many a
baneful herb and flower day by day, little by little,
until they silently gather a festering mass of corruption in their own soul. Let our artists rather be
those who are gifted to discern the true nature of
the beautiful and graceful: then will our youth
dwell in a land of health, amid fair sights and
sounds, and receive the good in everything; and
beauty, and effluence of fair works, shall flow into
the eye and ear, like a health-giving breeze from a
purer region, and insensibly draw the soul from
earliest years into likeness and sympathy with the
beauty of reason.'

" 'There can be no nobler training than that,' he
replied.

" 'And therefore,' I said, 'Glaucon, musical training is a more potent instrument than any other,
because rhythm and harmony find their way into
the inward places of the soul, on which they mightily
fasten, imparting grace, and making the soul of
him who is rightly educated graceful, or of him
who is ill-educated ungraceful; and also because
he who has received this true education of the
inner being will most shrewdly perceive omissions
or faults in art and nature, and with a true taste,
while he praises and rejoices over and receives into
his soul the good, and becomes noble and good, he
will justly blame and hate the bad, now in the
days of his youth, even before he is able to
know the reason why: and when reason comes he
will recognize and salute the friend with whom

his education has made him long familiar.' " [1]

This fusion of the ideas of the beautiful and the good is the central point in the Greek Theory of Art; and it enables us to understand how it was that they conceived art to be educational. Its end, in their view, was not only pleasure, though pleasure was essential to it; but also, and just as much, edification. Plato, indeed, here again exaggerating the current view, puts the edification above the pleasure. He criticizes Homer as he might criticize a moral philosopher, pointing out the inadequacy, from an ethical point of view, of his conception of heaven and of the gods, and dismissing as injurious and of bad example to youthful citizens the whole tissue of passionate human feeling, the irrepressible outbursts of anger and grief and fear, by virtue of which alone the Iliad and the Odyssey are immortal poems instead of ethical tracts. And finally, with a half reluctant assent to the course of his own argument, he excludes the poets altogether from his ideal republic, on the ground that they encourage their hearers in that indulgence of emotion which it is the object of every virtuous man to repress. The conclusion of Plato, by his own admission, was half paradoxical, and it certainly never recommended itself to such a nation of artists as the Greeks. But it illustrates, nevertheless, the general bent of their views of art, that tendency to the identification of the beautiful and the good, which, while it was never

[1] Plato, Republic III. 401.—Translated by Jowett.

pushed so far as to choke art with didactics—for Plato himself, even against his own will, is a poet—yet served to create a standard of taste which was ethical as much as æsthetic, and made the judgment of beauty also a judgment of moral worth.

Quite in accordance with this view we find that the central aim of all Greek art is the representation of human character and human ideals. The interpretation of "nature" for its own sake (in the narrower sense in which "nature" is opposed to man) is a modern and romantic development that would have been unintelligible to a Greek. Not that the Greeks were without a sense of what we call the beauties of nature, but that they treat them habitually, not as the centre of interest, but as the background to human activity. The most beautiful descriptions of nature to be found in Greek poetry occur, incidentally only, in the choral odes introduced into their dramas; and among all their pictures of which we have any record there is not one that answers to the description of a landscape; the subject is always mythological or historical, and the representation of nature merely a setting for the main theme. And on the other hand, the art for which the Greeks are most famous, and in which they have admittedly excelled all other peoples, is that art of sculpture whose special function it is not only to represent but to idealize the human form, and which is peculiarly adapted to embody for the sense not only physical but ethical types. And, more remarkable still, as we shall have occasion to observe later, the very art which modern men regard as the most devoid of all intellectual content, the most incommensurable with any standard except that of pure beauty—I refer of course to the art of music—was invested by the Greeks with a definite moral content and worked into their general theory of art as a direct interpretation of human life.   The excellence of man, in short, directly or indirectly, was the point about which Greek art turned; that excellence was at once æsthetic and ethical; and the representation of what was beautiful involved also the representation of what was good.   This point we will now proceed to illustrate more in detail in connection with the various special branches of art.

§ 3. Sculpture and Painting

Let us take, first, the plastic arts, sculpture and painting; and to bring into clear relief the Greek point of view let us contrast with it that of the modern "impressionist."   To the impressionist a picture is simply an arrangement of colour and line; the subject represented is nothing, the treatment everything.   It would be better, on the whole, not even to know what objects are depicted; and, to judge the picture by a comparison with the objects, or to consider what is the worth of the objects in themselves, or what we might think of them if we came across them in the connections of ordinary life, is simply to misconceive the whole meaning of a picture.   For the artist and for the man who understands art, all scales and standards disappear ex-

cept that of the purely æsthetic beauty which consists in harmony of line and tone; the most perfect
human form has no more value than a splash of
mud; or rather both mud and human form disappear as irrelevant, and all that is left for judgment is the arrangement of colour and form origi-
nally suggested by those accidental and indifferent
phenomena.

In the Greek view, on the other hand, though
we certainly cannot say that the subject was everything and the treatment nothing (for that would
be merely the annihilation of art) yet we may assert
that, granted the treatment, granted that the work
was beautiful (the first and indispensable require-
ment), its worth was determined by the character
of the subject. Sculpture and painting, in fact,
to the Greeks, were not merely a medium of
æsthetic pleasure; they were ways of expressing
and interpreting national life. As such they were
subordinated to religion. The primary end of
sculpture was to make statues of the gods and
heroes; the primary end of painting was to represent mythological scenes; and in either case the
purely æsthetic pleasure was also a means to a religious experience.

Let us take, for example, the statue of Zeus at
Olympia, the most famous of the works of Pheidias.
This colossal figure of ivory and gold was doubt-
less, according to all the testimony we possess, from
a merely æsthetic point of view, among the most
consummate creations of human genius. But what
was the main aim of the artist who made it? what

the main effect on the spectator? The artist had designed and the spectator seemed to behold a concrete image of that Homeric Zeus who was the centre of his religious consciousness—the Zeus who "nodded his dark brow, and the ambrosial locks waved from the King's immortal head, and he made great Olympus quake." [1] "Those who approach the temple," said Lucian, "do not conceive that they see ivory from the Indies or gold from the mines of Thrace; no, but the very son of Kronos and Rhea, transported by Pheidias to earth and set to watch over the lonely plain of Pisa." "He was," says Dion Chrysostom, "the type of that unattained ideal, Hellas come to unity with herself; in expression at once mild and awful, as befits the giver of life and all good gifts, the common father, saviour and guardian of men; dignified as a king, tender as a father, awful as giver of laws, kind as protector of suppliants and friends, simple and great as giver of increase and wealth; revealing, in a word, in form and countenance, the whole array of gifts and qualities proper to his supreme divinity."

The description is characteristic of the whole aim of Greek sculpture,—the representation not only of beauty, but of character, not only of character, but of character idealized. The statues of the various gods derive their distinguishing individuality not merely from their association with conventional symbols, but from a concrete reproduction, in features, expression, drapery, pose, of the ethical and

[1] Iliad. I. 528.—Translated by Lang, Leaf and Myers.

intellectual qualities for which they stand. An
Apollo differs in type from a Zeus, an Athene from
a Demeter; and in every case the artist works from
an intellectual conception, bent not simply on a
graceful harmony of lines, but on the representation of a character at once definite and ideal.

Primarily, then, Greek sculpture was an expression of the national religion; and therefore,
also, of the national life. For, as we saw, the cult
of the gods was the centre, not only of the religious but of the political consciousness of Greece;
and an art which was born and flourished in the
temple and the sacred grove, naturally became the
exponent of the ideal aspect of the state. It was
thus, for example, that the Parthenon at Athens
was at once the centre of the worship of Athene,
and a symbol of the corporate life over which she
presided; the statue of the goddess having as its
appropriate complement the frieze over which the
spirit of the city moved in stone. And thus, too,
the statues of the victors at the Olympian games
were dedicated in the sacred precinct, as a memorial
of what was not only an athletic meeting, but also
at once a centre of Hellenic unity and the most
consummate expression of that aspect of their culture which contributed at least as much to their
æsthetic as to their physical perfection.

Sculpture, in fact, throughout, was subordinated
to religion, and through religion to national life; and
it was from this that it derived its ideal and intellectual character. And, so far as our authorities enable us to judge, the same is true of painting.

The great pictures of which we have descriptions were painted to adorn temples and public buildings, and represented either mythological or national themes. Such, for example, was the great work of Polygnotus at Delphi, in which was depicted on the one hand the sack of Troy, on the other the descent of Odysseus into Hades; and such his representation of the battle of Marathon, in the painted porch that led to the Acropolis of Athens. And even the vase paintings, of which we have innumerable examples, and which are mere decorations of common domestic utensils, have often enough some story of gods and heroes for their theme, whereby over and above their purely æsthetic value they made their appeal to the general religious consciousness of Greece. Painting, like sculpture, had its end, in a sense, outside itself; and from this very fact derived its peculiar dignity, simplicity, and power.

From this account of the plastic art of the Greeks it follows as a simple corollary, that their aim was not merely to reproduce but to transcend nature. For their subject was gods and heroes, and heroes and gods were superior to men. Of this idealizing tendency we have in sculpture evidence enough in the many examples which have been preserved to us; and with regard to painting there is curious literary testimony to the same effect. Aristotle, for example, remarks that "even if it is impossible that men should be such as Zeuxis painted them, yet it is better that he should paint them so; for the example ought to excel that for which it is an

example." [1] And in an imaginary conversation
recorded between Socrates and Parrhasius the artist
admits without any hesitation that more pleasure
is to be derived from pictures of men who are
morally good than from those of men who are morally bad. In the Greek view, in fact, as we saw,
physical and moral excellence went together, and
it was excellence they sought to depict in their art;
not merely æsthetic beauty, though that was a
necessary presupposition, but on the top of that,
ideal types of character representative of their conception of the hero and the god. Art, in a word,
was subordinate to the ethical ideal; or rather the
ethical and æsthetic ideals were not yet dissociated;
and the greatest artists the world has ever known
worked deliberately under the direction and inspiration of the ideas that controlled and determined the life of their time.

§ 4. Music and the Dance

Turning now from the plastic arts to that other
group which the Greeks classed together under the
name of "Music"—namely music, in the narrower
sense, dancing and poetry—we find still more clearly
emphasized and more elaborately worked out the
subordination of æsthetic to ethical and religious
ends. "Music," in fact, as they used the term,
was the centre of Greek education, and its moral
character thus became a matter of primary importance. By it were formed, it was supposed, the

[1] Arist. Poet. XXV., 1461, 6. 12.

mind and temper of the citizens, and so the whole constitution of the state. "The introduction of a new kind of music," says Plato, "must be shunned as imperilling the whole state; since styles of music are never disturbed without affecting the most important political institutions." "The new style," he goes on, "gradually gaining a lodgment, quietly insinuates itself into manners and customs; and from these it issues in greater force, and makes its way into mutual compacts; and from compacts it goes on to attack laws and constitutions, displaying the utmost impudence, until it ends by overturning everything, both in public and in private." [1] And as in his Republic he had defined the character of the poetry that should be admitted into his ideal state, so in the "Laws" he specially defines the character of the melodies and dances, regarding them as the most important factor in determining and preserving the manners and institutions of the citizens.

Nothing, at first sight, to a modern mind, could be stranger than this point of view. That poetry has a bearing on conduct we can indeed understand, though we do not make poetry the centre of our system of education; but that moral effects should be attributed to music and to dancing, and that these should be regarded as of such importance as to influence profoundly the whole constitution of a state, will appear to the majority of modern men an unintelligible paradox.

[1] Plato, Rep. IV., 424 c.—Translated by Davies and Vaughan.

Yet no opinion of the Greeks is more profoundly characteristic than this of their whole way of regarding life, and none would better repay a careful study. That moral character should be attributed to the influence of music is only one and perhaps the most striking illustration of that general identification by the Greeks of the ethical and the æsthetic standards on which we have so frequently had occasion to insist. Virtue, in their conception, was not a hard conformity to a law felt as alien to the natural character; it was the free expression of a beautiful and harmonious soul. And this very metaphor "harmonious," which they so constantly employ, involves the idea of a close connection between music and morals. Character, in the Greek view, is a certain proportion of the various elements of the soul, and the right character is the right proportion. But the relation in which these elements stand to one another could be directly affected, it was found, by means of music; not only could the different emotions be excited or assuaged in various degrees, but the whole relation of the emotional to the rational element could be regulated and controlled by the appropriate melody and measure. That this connection between music and morals really does exist is recognized, in a rough and general way, by most people who have any musical sense. There are rhythms and tunes, for example, that are felt to be vulgar and base, and others that are felt to be ennobling; some music, Wagner's, for instance, is frequently called immoral; Gounod is described as enervating, Beethoven as bracing, and the like; and however absurd such comments may often appear to be in detail, underlying them is the undoubtedly well-grounded sense that various kinds of music have various ethical qualities. But it is just this side of music, which has been neglected in modern times, that was the one on which the Greeks laid most stress. Infinitely inferior to the moderns in the mechanical resources of the art, they had made, it appears, a far finer and closer analysis of its relation to emotional states; with the result that even in music, which we describe as the purest of the arts, congratulating ourselves on its absolute dissociation from all definite intellectual conceptions,—even here the standard of the Greeks was as much ethical as æsthetic, and the style of music was distinguished and its value appraised, not only by the pleasure to be derived from it, but also by the effect it tended to produce on character.

Of this position we have a clear and definite statement in Aristotle. Virtue, he says, consists in loving and hating in the proper way, and implies, therefore, a delight in the proper emotions; but emotions of any kind are produced by melody and rhythm; therefore by music a man becomes accustomed to feeling the right emotions. Music has thus the power to form character; and the various kinds of music, based on the various modes, may be distinguished by their effects on character—one, for example, working in the direction of melancholy, another of effeminacy; one encouraging abandonment, another self-control, another enthusiasm, and so on through the series. It follows that music may be judged not merely by the pleasure it gives, but by the character of its moral influence; pleasure, indeed, is essential or there would be no art; but the different kinds of pleasure given by different kinds of music are to be distinguished not merely by quantity, but by quality.   One will produce a right pleasure of which the good man will approve, and which will have a good effect on character, another will be in exactly the opposite case.   Or, as Plato puts it, "the excellence of music is to be measured by pleasure.   But the pleasure must not be that of chance persons; the fairest music is that which delights the best and best educated, and especially that which delights the one man who is pre-eminent in virtue and education." [1]

We see then that even pure music, to the Greeks, had a distinct and definite ethical bearing.   But this ethical influence was further emphasized by the fact that it was not their custom to enjoy their music pure.   What they called "music," as has been already pointed out, was an intimate union of melody, verse and dance, so that the particular emotional meaning of the rhythm and tune employed was brought out into perfect lucidity by the accompanying words and gestures.   Thus we find, for example, that Plato characterizes a tendency in his own time to the separation of melody and verse as a sign of a want of true artistic taste; for, he says, it is very hard, in the absence of words, to distinguish the exact character of the mood which the rhythm and

[1] Plato, Laws, II. 658 e.—Translated by Jowett.

tune is supposed to represent. In this connection it may be interesting to refer to the use of the *"leit-motiv"* in modern music. Here too a particular idea, if not a particular set of words, is associated with the particular musical phrase; the intention of the practice being clearly the same as that which is indicated in the passage just quoted, namely to add precision and definiteness to the vague emotional content of pure music.

And this determining effect of words was further enhanced, in the music of the Greeks, by the additional accompaniment of the dance. The emotional character conveyed to the mind by the words and to the ear by the tune, was further explained to the eye by gesture, pose, and beat of foot; the combination of the three modes of expression forming thus in the Greek sense a single "imitative" art. The dance as well as the melody came thus to have a definite ethical significance; "it imitates," says Aristotle, "character, emotion, and action." And Plato in his ideal republic would regulate by law the dances no less than the melodies to be employed, distinguishing them too as morally good or morally bad, and encouraging the one while he forbids the other.

The general Greek view of music which has thus been briefly expounded, the union of melody and rhythm with poetry and the dance in view of a definite and consciously intended ethical character, may be illustrated by the following passage of Plutarch, in which he describes the music in vogue at Sparta. The whole system, it will be observed,

is designed with a view to that military courage
which was the virtue most prized in the Spartan
state, and the one about which all their institutions
centred.   Music at Sparta actually was, what Plato
would have had it in his ideal republic, a public and
state-regulated function; and even that vigorous
race which of all the Greeks came nearest to being
Philistines of virtue, thought fit to lay a foundation
purely æsthetic for their severe and soldierly ideal.

"Their instruction in music and verse," says
Plutarch, "was not less carefully attended to than
their habits of grace and good-breeding in conversation.   And their very songs had a life and spirit in
them that inflamed and possessed men's minds with
an enthusiasm and ardour for action; the style of
them was plain and without affectation; the subject
always serious and moral; most usually, it was in
praise of such men as had died in defence of their
country, or in derision of those that had been
cowards; the former they declared happy and
glorified; the life of the latter they described as
most miserable and abject.   There were also vaunts
of what they would do and boasts of what they had
done, varying with the various ages; as, for example,
they had three choirs in their solemn festivals, the
first of the old men, the second of the young men,
and the last of the children; the old men began
thus:

" 'We once were young and brave and strong;'

the young men answering them, singing:

" 'And we're so now, come on and try:'

the children came last and said:

" 'But we'll be strongest by-and-by.'

"Indeed, if we will take the pains to consider their compositions, and the airs on the flute to which they marched when going to battle, we shall find that Terpander and Pindar had reason to say that music and valour were allied." [1]

The way of regarding music which is illustrated in this passage, and in all that is said on the subject by Greek writers, is so typical of the whole point of view of the Greeks, that we may be pardoned for insisting once again on the attitude of mind which it implies.   Music, as we saw, had an ethical value to the Greeks; but that is not to say that they put the ethics first, and the music second, using the one as a mere tool of the other.   Rather an ethical state of mind was also, in their view, a musical one.   In a sense something more than metaphorical, virtue was a harmony of the soul.   The musical end was thus identical with the ethical one.   The most beautiful music was also the morally best, and *vice versa;* virtue was not prior to beauty, nor beauty to virtue; they were two aspects of the same reality, two ways of regarding a single fact; and if æsthetic effects were supposed to be amenable to ethical judgment, it was only because ethical judgments at bottom

[1] Plutarch, "Lycurgus," ch. 21 (Clough's Edition).

were æsthetic. The "good" and the "beautiful" were one and the same thing; that is the first and last word of the Greek ideal.

And while thus, on the one hand, virtue was invested with the spontaneity and delight of art, on the other, art derived from its association with ethics emotional precision. In modern times the end of music is commonly conceived to be simply and without more ado the excitement of feeling. Its value is measured by the intensity rather than the quality of the emotion which it is capable of arousing; and the auditor abandons himself to a casual succession of highly wrought moods as bewildering in the actual experience as it is exhausting in the after-effects. In Greek music, on the other hand, if we may trust our accounts, while the intensity of the feeling excited must have been far less than that which it is in the power of modern instrumentation to evoke, its character was perfectly simple and definite. Melody, rhythm, gesture and words, were all consciously adapted to the production of a single precisely conceived emotional effect; the listener was in a position clearly to understand and appraise the value of the mood excited in him; instead of being exhausted and confused by a chaos of vague and conflicting emotion he had the sense of relief which accompanies the deliverance of a definite passion, and returned to his ordinary business "purged," as they said, and tranquillized, by a process which he understood, directed to an end of which he approved.

§ 5. POETRY

If now, as we have seen, in the plastic arts, and in an art which appears to us so pure as music, the Greeks perceived and valued, along with the immediate pleasure of beauty, a definite ethical character and bent, much more was this the case with poetry, whose material is conceptions and ideas. The works of the poets, and especially of Homer, were in fact to the Greeks all that moral treatises are to us; or rather, instead of learning their lessons in abstract terms, they learnt them out of the concrete representation of life. Poetry was the basis of their education, the guide and commentary of their practice, the inspiration of their speculative thought. If they have a proposition to advance, they must back it by a citation: if they have a counsel to offer, they must prop it with a verse. Not only for delight, but for inspiration, warning and example, they were steeped from childhood onwards in an ocean of melodious discourse; their national epics were to them what the Bible was to the Puritans; and for every conjunction of fortune, for every issue of home or state, they found therein a text to prompt or reinforce their decision. Of this importance of poetry in the life of ancient Greece, and generally of the importance of music and art, the following passage from Plato is a striking illustration: "When the boy has learned his letters and is beginning to understand what is written, as before he understood only what was spoken, they put into his hands the works of great poets, which he reads at school; in these are contained many admonitions, and many tales, and praises, and encomia of ancient famous men, which he is required to learn by heart, in order that he may imitate or emulate them and desire to become like them.   Then again the teachers of the lyre take similar care that their young disciple is temperate and gets into no mischief; and when they have taught him the use of the lyre, they introduce him to the poems of other excellent poets, who are the lyric poets; and these they set to music and make their harmonies and rhythms quite familiar to the children's souls, in order that they may learn to be more gentle and harmonious and rhythmical, and so more fitted for speech and action; for the life of man in every part has need of harmony and rhythm." [1]

From this conception of poetry as a storehouse of practical wisdom the transition is easy to a purely ethical judgment of its value; and that transition, as has been already noted, was actually made by Plato, who even goes so far as to prescribe to poets the direct inculcation of such morals as are proper to a tract, as that the good and just man is happy even though he be poor, and the bad and unjust man miserable even though he be rich.   This didacticism, no doubt, is a parody; but it is a parody of the normal Greek view, that the excellence of a poem is closely bound up with the compass and depth of its whole ethical content, and is not to be measured, as

[1] Plato, Prot., 325 c.—Translated by Jowett.

many moderns maintain, merely by the æsthetic beauty of its form. When Strabo says, "it is impossible to be a good poet unless you are first a good man," he is expressing the common opinion of the Greeks that the poet is to be judged not merely as an artist but as an interpreter of life; and the same pre-supposition underlies the remark of Aristotle that poets may be classified according as the characters they represent are as good as, better, or worse than the average man.

But perhaps the most remarkable illustration of this way of regarding poetry is the passage in the "Frogs" of Aristophanes, where the comedian has introduced a controversy between Æschylus and Euripides as to the relative merit of their works, and has made the decision turn almost entirely on moral considerations, the question being really whether or no Euripides is to be regarded as a corrupter of his countrymen. In the course of the discussion Æschylus is made to give expression to a view of poetry which clearly enough Aristophanes endorses himself, and which no doubt would be accepted by the majority of his audience. He appeals to all antiquity to show that poets have always been the instructors of mankind, and that it is for this that they are held in honour.

> "Look to traditional history, look
> To antiquity, primitive, early, remote;
> See there, what a blessing illustrious poets
> Conferr'd on mankind, in the centuries past.
> Orpheus instructed mankind in religion,
> Reclaim'd them from bloodshed and barbarous rites;

Musaeus deliver'd the doctrine of med'cine,
And warnings prophetic for ages to come;
Next came old Hesiod, teaching us husbandry,
Ploughing, and sowing, and rural affairs,
Rural economy, rural astronomy,
Homely morality, labour, and thrift;
Homer himself, our adorable Homer,
What was his title to praise and renown?
What, but the worth of the lessons he taught us,
Discipline, arms, and equipment of war?" [1]

While, then, there is, as we should naturally expect, plenty of Greek poetry which is simply the spontaneous expression of passionate feeling, unrestrained by the consideration of ethical or other ends; yet if we take for our type (as we are fairly entitled to do, from the prominent place it held in Greek life), not the lyrics but the drama of Greece, we shall find that in poetry even (as was to be expected) to a higher degree than in music and the plastic arts, the beauty sought and achieved is one that lies within the limits of certain definite moral pre-suppositions. Let us consider this point in some detail; and first let us examine the character of Greek tragedy.

§ 6. TRAGEDY

The character of Greek tragedy was determined from the very beginning by the fact of its connection with religion. The season at which it was performed was the festival of Dionysius; about his al-

[1] Aristoph., Frogs, 1030.—Translated by Frere.

tar the chorus danced; and the object of the performance was the representation of scenes out of
the lives of ancient heroes. The subject of the
drama was thus strictly prescribed; it must be selected out of a cycle of legends familiar to the audience; and whatever freedom might be allowed to
the poet in his treatment of the theme, whatever the
reflections he might embroider upon it, the speculative or ethical views, the criticism of contemporary
life, all must be subservient to the main object orig-
inally proposed, the setting forth, for edification as
well as for delight, of some episodes in the lives of
those heroes of the past who were considered not
only to be greater than their descendants, but to be
the sons of gods and worthy themselves of worship
as divine.

By this fundamental condition the tragedy of the
Greeks is distinguished sharply, on the one hand
from the Shakespearian drama, on the other from
the classical drama of the French. The tragedies
of Shakespeare are devoid, one might say, or at
least comparatively devoid, of all preconceptions.
He was free to choose what subject he liked and to
treat it as he would; and no sense of obligation to
religious or other points of view, no feeling for traditions descended from a sacred past and not lightly
to be handled by those who were their trustees for
the future, sobered or restrained for evil or for good
his half-barbaric genius. He flung himself upon life
with the irresponsible ardour of the discoverer of a
new continent; shaped and re-shaped it as he chose,
carved from it now the cynicism of Measure for

Measure, now the despair of Hamlet and of Lear, now the radiant magnanimity of the Tempest, and departed leaving behind him not a map or chart, but a series of mutually incompatible landscapes.

What Shakespeare gave, in short, was a many-sided representation of life; what the Greek drama-tist gave was an interpretation. But an interpreta-tion not simply personal to himself, but representa-tive of the national tradition and belief. The men whose deeds and passions he narrated were the pat-terns and examples on the one hand, on the other the warnings of his race; the gods who determined the fortunes they sang, were working still among men; the moral laws that ruled the past ruled the present too; and the history of the Hellenic race moved, under a visible providence, from its divine origin onward to an end that would be prosperous or the reverse according as later generations should con-tinue to observe the worship and traditions of their fathers descended from heroes and gods.

And it is the fact that in this sense it was repre-sentative of the national consciousness, that distin-guishes the Greek tragedy from the classical drama of the French. For the latter, though it imitated the ancients in outward form, was inspired with a totally different spirit. The kings and heroes whose fortunes it narrated were not the ancestors of the French race; they had no root in its affections, no connection with its religious beliefs, no relation to its ethical conceptions. The whole ideal set forth was not that which really inspired the nation, but at best that which was supposed to inspire the court; and the whole drama, like a tree transplanted to an alien soil, withers and dies for lack of the nourishment which the tragedy of the Greeks unconsciously imbibed from its encompassing air of national tradition.

Such, then, was the general character of the Greek tragedy—an interpretation of the national ideal. Let us now proceed to follow out some of the consequences involved in this conception.

In the first place, the theme represented is the life and fate of ancient heroes—of personages, that is to say, greater than ordinary men, both for good and for evil, in their qualities and in their achievements, pregnant with fateful issues, makers or marrers of the fortunes of the world. Tragic and terrible their destiny may be, but never contemptible or squalid. Behind all suffering, behind sin and crime, must lie a redeeming magnanimity. A complete villain, says Aristotle, is not a tragic character, for he has no hold upon the sympathies; if he prosper, it is an outrage on common human feeling; if he fall into disaster, it is merely what he deserves. Neither is it admissible to represent the misfortunes of a thoroughly good man, for that is merely painful and distressing; and least of all is it tolerable gratuitously to introduce mere baseness, or madness, or other aberrations from human nature. The true tragic hero is a man of high place and birth who having a nature not ignoble has fallen into sin and pays in suffering the penalty of his act. Nothing could throw more light on the distinguishing characteristics of the Greek drama than these few remarks of Aristotle, and nothing could better indicate how close, in the Greek mind, was the connection between æsthetic and ethical judgments. The canon of Aristotle would exclude as proper themes for tragedy the character and fate, say, of Richard III.—the absolutely bad man suffering his appropriate desert; or of Kent and Cordelia—the absolutely good, brought into unmerited affliction; and that not merely because such themes offend the moral sense, but because by so offending they destroy the proper pleasure of the tragic art. The whole æsthetic effect is limited by ethical pre-suppositions; and to outrage these is to defeat the very purpose of tragedy.

Specially interesting in this connection are the strictures passed on Euripides in the passage of the "Frogs" of Aristophanes to which allusion has already been made. Euripides is there accused of lowering the tragic art by introducing—what? Women in love! The central theme of modern tragedy! It is the boast of Æschylus that there is not one of his plays which touches on this subject:

"I never allow'd of your lewd Sthenoboeas
  Or filthy detestable Phaedras—not I!
  Indeed I should doubt if my drama throughout
  Exhibit an instance of woman in love!" [1]

And there can be little doubt that with a Greek audience this would count to him as a merit, and that the shifting of the centre of interest by Euripides from the sterner passions of heroes and of

[1] Aristoph. Frogs, 1043.—Translated by Frere.

kings to this tenderer phase of human feeling would
be felt even by those whom it charmed to be a de-
clension from the height of the older tragedy.

And to this limitation of subject corresponds a
limitation of treatment. The Greek tragedy is composed from a definite point of view, with the aim not
merely to represent but also to interpret the theme.
Underlying the whole construction of the plot, the
dialogue, the reflections, the lyric interludes, is the
intention to illustrate some general moral law, some
common and typical problem, some fundamental
truth. Of the elder dramatists at any rate, Æschylus and Sophocles, one may even say that it was their
purpose—however imperfectly achieved—to "justify
the ways of God to man." To represent suffering as
the punishment of sin is the constant bent of Æschylus; to justify the law of God against the presump-
tion of man is the central idea of Sophocles. In
either case the whole tone is essentially religious.
To choose such a theme as Lear, to treat it as
Shakespeare has treated it, to leave it, as it were,
bleeding from a thousand wounds, in mute and help-
less entreaty for the healing that is never to be
vouchsafed—this would have been repulsive, if not
impossible, to a Greek tragedian. Without ever de-
scending from concrete art to the abstractions of
mere moralizing, without ever attempting to substitute a verbal formula for the full and complex perception that grows out of a representation of life,
the ancient dramatists were nevertheless, in the
whole apprehension of their theme, determined by a
more or less conscious speculative bias; the world

to them was not merely a splendid chaos, it was a divine plan; and even in its darkest hollows, its passes most perilous and bleak, they have their hand, though doubtful perhaps and faltering, upon the clue that is to lead them up to the open sky.

It is consonant with this account of the nature of Greek tragedy that it should have laid more stress upon action than upon character. The interest was centred on the universal bearing of certain acts and situations, on the light which the experience represented threw on the whole tendency and course of human life, not on the sentiments and motives of the particular personages introduced. The characters are broad and simple, not developing for the most part, but fixed, and fitted therefore to be the mediums of direct action, for simple issues, and typical situations. In the Greek tragedy the general point of view predominates over the idiosyncrasies of particular persons. It is human nature that is represented in the broad, not this or that highly specialized variation; and what we have indicated as the general aim, the interpretation of life, is never obscured by the predominance of exceptional and, so to speak, accidental characteristics. Man is the subject of the Greek drama; the subject of the modern novel is Tom and Dick.

Finally, to the realization of this general aim, the whole form of the Greek drama was admirably adapted. It consisted very largely of conversations between two persons, representing two opposed points of view, and giving occasion for an almost scientific discussion of every problem of action raised in the play; and between these conversations were inserted lyric odes in which the chorus commented on the situation, bestowed advice or warning, praise or blame, and finally summed up the moral of the whole. Through the chorus, in fact, the poet could speak in his own person, and impose upon the whole tragedy any tone which he desired. Periodically he could drop the dramatist and assume the preacher; and thus ensure that his play should be, what we have seen was its recognized ideal, not merely a representation but an interpretation of life.

But this without ceasing to be a work of art. In attempting to analyze in abstract terms the general character of the Greek tragedy we have necessarily thrown into the shade what after all was its primary and most essential aspect; an aspect, however, of which a full appreciation could only be attained not by a mere perusal of the text, but by what is unfortunately for ever beyond our power, the witnessing of an actual representation as it was given on the Greek stage. For from a purely æsthetic point of view the Greek drama must be reckoned among the most perfect of art forms.

Taking place in the open air, on the sunny slope of a hill, valley and plain or islanded sea stretching away below to meet the blazing blue of a cloudless sky, the moving pageant, thus from the first set in tune with nature, brought to a focus of splendour the rays of every separate art. More akin to an opera than to a play, it had, as its basis, music. For the drama had developed out of the lyric ode, and retained throughout what was at first its only element, the dance and song of a mimetic chorus. By this centre of rhythmic motion and pregnant melody the burden of the tale was caught up and echoed and echoed again, as the living globe divided into spheres of answering song, the clear and precise significance of the plot, never obscure to the head, being thus brought home in music to the passion of the heart, the idea embodied in lyric verse, the verse transfigured by song, and song and verse reflected as in a mirror to the eye by the swing and beat of the limbs they stirred to consonance of motion. And while such was the character of the odes that broke the action of the play, the action itself was an appeal not less to the ear and to the eye than to the passion and the intellect. The circumstances of the representation, the huge auditorium in the open air, lent themselves less to "acting" in our sense of the term, than to attitude and declamation. The actors raised on high boots above their natural height, their faces hidden in masks and their tones mechanically magnified, must have relied for their effects not upon facial play, or rapid and subtle variations of voice and gesture, but upon a certain statuesque beauty of pose, and a chanting intonation of that majestic iambic verse whose measure would have been ob-scured by a rapid and conversational delivery. The representation would thus become moving sculpture to the eye, and to the ear, as it were, a sleep of music between the intenser interludes of the chorus; and the spectator without being drawn away by an imitative realism from the calm of impassioned con-templation into the fever and fret of a veritable

actor on the scene, received an impression based
throughout on that clear intellectual foundation,
that almost prosaic lucidity of sentiment and plot,
which is preserved to us in the written text, but
raised by the accompanying appeal to the sense,
made as it must have been made by such artists as
the Greeks, by the grouping of forms and colours,
the recitative, the dance and the song, to such a
greatness and height of æsthetic significance as can
hardly have been realized by any other form of art
production.

The nearest modern analogy to what the ancient
drama must have been is to be found probably in the
operas of Wagner, who indeed was strongly in-
fluenced by the tragedy of the Greeks.   It was his
ideal, like theirs, to combine the various branches of
art, employing not only music but poetry, sculpture,
painting and the dance, for the representation of his
dramatic theme; and his conception also to make
art the interpreter of life, reflecting in a national
drama the national consciousness, the highest action
and the deepest passion and thought of the German
race.   To consider how far in this attempt he falls
short of or goes beyond the achievement of the
Greeks, and to examine the wide dissimilarities that
underlie the general identity of aim, would be to
wander too far afield from our present theme.   But
the comparison may be recommended to those who
are anxious to form a concrete idea of what the effect
of a Greek tragedy may have been, and to clothe in
imagination the dead bones of the literary text with
the flesh and blood of a representation to the sense.

Meantime, to assist the reader to realize with somewhat greater precision the bearing of the foregoing remarks, it may be worth while to give an outline sketch of one of the most celebrated of the Greek tragedies, the "Agamemnon" of Æschylus.

The hero of the drama belongs to that heroic house whose tragic history was among the most terrible and the most familiar to a Greek audience. Tantalus, the founder of the family, for some offence against the gods, was suffering in Hades the punishment which is christened by his name. His son Pelops was stained with the blood of Myrtilus. Of the two sons of the next generation, Thyestes seduced the wife of his brother Atreus; and Atreus in return killed the sons of Thyestes, and made the father unwittingly eat the flesh of the murdered boys. Agamemnon, son of Atreus, to propitiate Artemis, sacrificed his daughter Iphigenia, and in revenge was murdered by Clytemnestra, his wife. And Clytemnestra was killed by Orestes, her son, in atonement for the death of Agamemnon. For generations the race had been dogged by crime and punishment; and in choosing for his theme the murder of Agamemnon the dramatist could assume in his audience so close a familiarity with the past history of the House that he could call into existence by an allusive word that sombre background of woe to enhance the terrors of his actual presentation. The figures he brought into vivid relief joined hands with menacing forms that faded away into the night of the future and the past; while above them hung, intoning doom, the phantom host of Furies.

Yet at the outset of the drama all promises well. The watchman on the roof of the palace, in the tenth year of his watch, catches sight at last of the signal fire that announces the capture of Troy and the speedy return of Agamemnon. With joy he proclaims to the House the long-delayed and welcome news; yet even in the moment of exultation lets slip a doubtful phrase hinting at something behind, which he dares not name, something which may turn to despair the triumph of victory. Hereupon enter the chorus of Argive elders, chanting as they move to the measure of a stately march. They sing how ten years before Agamemnon and Menelaus had led forth the host of Greece, at the bidding of the Zeus who protects hospitality, to recover for Menelaus Helen his wife, treacherously stolen by Paris. Then, as they take their places and begin their rhythmic dance, in a strain of impassioned verse that is at once a narrative and a lyric hymn, they tell, or rather, present in a series of vivid images, flashing as by illumination of lightning out of a night of veiled and sombre boding, the tale of the deed that darkened the starting of the host—the sacrifice of Iphigenia to the goddess whose wrath was delaying the fleet at Aulis. In verse, in music, in pantomime, the scene lives again—the struggle in the father's heart, the insistence of his brother chiefs, the piteous glance of the girl, and at last the unutterable end; while above and through it all rings like a knell of fate the refrain that is the motive of the whole drama:

"Sing woe, sing woe, but may the Good prevail."

At the conclusion of the ode enters Clytemnestra. She makes a formal announcement to the chorus of the fall of Troy; describes the course of the signal-fire from beacon to beacon as it sped, and pictures in imagination the scenes even then taking place in the doomed city. On her withdrawal the chorus break once more into song and dance. To the music of a solemn hymn they point the moral of the fall of Troy, the certain doom of violence and fraud descended upon Paris and his House. Once more the vivid pictures flash from the night of woe—Helen in her fatal beauty stepping lightly to her doom, the widower's nights of mourning haunted by the ghost of love, the horrors of the war that followed, the slain abroad and the mourners at home, the change of living flesh and blood for the dust and ashes of the tomb. At last with a return to their original theme, the doom of insolence, the chorus close their ode and announce the arrival of a messenger from Troy. Talthybius, the herald, enters as spokesman of the army and King, describing the hardships they have suffered and the joy of the triumphant issue. To him Clytemnestra announces, in words of which the irony is patent to the audience, her sufferings in the absence of her husband and her delight at the prospect of his return. He will find her, she says, as he left her, a faithful watcher of the home, her loyalty sure, her honour undefiled. Then follows another choral ode, similar in theme to the last, dwelling on the woe brought by the act of Paris upon Troy, the change of the bridal song to the trump of war and the dirge of death; contrasting, in

a profusion of splendid tropes, the beauty of Helen
with the curse to which it is bound; and insisting
once more on the doom that attends insolence and
pride. At the conclusion of this song the measure
changes to a march, and the chorus turn to welcome
the triumphant king. Agamemnon enters, and behind him the veiled and silent figure of a woman.
After greeting the gods of his House, the King, in
brief and stilted phrase, acknowledges the loyalty
of the chorus, but hints at much that is amiss which
it must be his first charge to set right. Hereupon
enters Clytemnestra, and in a speech of rhetorical
exaggeration tells of her anxious waiting for her
lord and her inexpressible joy at his return. In
conclusion she directs that purple cloth be spread
upon his path that he may enter the house as befits
a conqueror. After a show of resistance, Agamemnon yields the point, and the contrast at which the
dramatist aims is achieved. With the pomp of an
eastern monarch, always repellent to the Greek
mind, the King steps across the threshold, steps, as
the audience knows, to his death. The higher the
reach of his power and pride the more terrible and
swift is the nemesis; and Clytemnestra follows in
triumph with the enigmatic cry upon her lips:
"Zeus, who art god of fulfilment, fulfil my prayers."
As she withdraws the chorus begin a song of boding
fear, the more terrible that it is still indefinite.
Something is going to happen—the presentiment is
sure. But what, but what? They search the night
in vain. Meantime, motionless and silent, waits the
figure of the veiled woman. It is Cassandra, the

prophetess, daughter of Priam of Troy, whom Agamemnon has carried home as his prize. Clytemnestra returns to urge her to enter the house; she
makes no sign and utters no word. The Queen
changes her tone from courtesy to anger and re-
buke; the figure neither stirs nor speaks; and Clytemnestra at last with an angry threat leaves her
and returns to the palace. Then, and not till then,
a cry breaks from the stranger's lips, a passionate
cry to Apollo who gave her her fatal gift. All the
sombre history of the House to which she had been
brought, the woe that has been and the woe that is
to come, passes in pictures across her inner sense.
In a series of broken ejaculations, not sentences but
lyric cries, she evokes the scenes of the past and of
the future. Blood drips from the palace; in its
chambers the Furies crouch; the murdered sons of
Thyestes wail in its haunted courts; and ever among
the visions of the past that one of the future floats
and fades, clearly discerned, impossible to avert, the
murder of a husband by a wife; and in the rear of
that, most pitiful of all, the violent death of the seer
who sees in vain and may not help. Between
Cassandra and the Chorus it is a duet of anguish
and fear; in the broken lyric phrases a phantom
music wails; till at last, at what seems the breaking-
point, the tension is relaxed, and dropping into the
calmer iambic recitative, Cassandra tells her message in plainer speech and clearly proclaims the
murder of the King. Then, with a last appeal to
the avenger that is to come, she enters the palace
alone to meet her death.—The stage is empty.

Suddenly a cry is heard from within; again, and
then again; while the chorus hesitate the deed is
done; the doors are thrown open, and Clytemnestra
is seen standing over the corpses of her victims.
All disguise is now thrown off; the murderess
avows and triumphs in her deed; she justifies it as
vengeance for the sacrifice of Iphigenia, and sees in
herself not a free human agent but the incarnate
curse of the House of Tantalus.   And now for the
first time appears the adulterer Ægisthus, who has
planned the whole behind the scenes.   He too is an
avenger, for he is the son of that Thyestes who was
made to feed on his own children's flesh.   The murder of Agamemnon is but one more link in the long
chain of hereditary guilt; and with that exposition
of the pitiless law of punishment and crime this
chapter of the great drama comes to a close.   But
the "Agamemnon" is only the first of a series of
three plays closely connected and meant to be performed in succession; and the problem raised in the
first of them, the crime that cries for punishment
and the punishment that is itself a new crime, is
solved in the last by a reconciliation of the powers
of heaven and hell, and the pardon of the last offender in the person of Orestes.   To sketch, however, the plan of the other dramas of the triology
would be to trespass too far upon our space and
time.   It is enough to have illustrated, by the example of the "Agamemnon," the general character
of a Greek tragedy; and those who care to pursue
the subject further must be referred to the text of
the plays themselves.

§ 7. COMEDY

Even more remarkable than the tragedy of the Greeks, in its rendering of a didactic intention under the forms of a free and spontaneous art, is the older comedy known to us through the works of Aristophanes. As the former dealt with the general conceptions, religious and ethical, that underlay the Greek view of life, using as its medium of exposition the ancient national myths, so the latter dealt with the particular phases of contemporary life, employing the machinery of a free burlesque. The achievement of Aristophanes, in fact, is more astonishing, in a sense, than that of Æschylus. Starting with what is always, *prima facie*, the prose of everyday life, its acrid controversies, its vulgar and tedious types, and even its particular individuals— for Aristophanes does not hesitate to introduce his contemporaries in person on the stage—he fits to this gross and heavy stuff the wings of imagination, scatters from it the clinging mists of banality and spite, and speeds it forth through the lucid heaven of art amid peals of musical laughter and snatches of lyric song. For Aristophanes was a poet as well as a comedian, and his genius is displayed not only in the construction of his fantastic plots, not only in the inexhaustible profusion of his humane and genial wit, but in bursts of pure poetry as melodious and inspired as ever sprang from the lips of the lyrists of Greece or of the world. The basis of the comic as of the tragic art of the Greeks was song

and dance; and the chorus, the original element of
the play, still retains in the works of Aristophanes
a place important enough to make it clear that in
comedy, too, a prominent aspect of the art must
have been the æsthetic appeal to the ear and the
eye. In general structure, in fact, comedy and
tragedy were alike; æsthetically the motives were
similar, only they were set in a different key.

But while primarily Aristophanes, like the trage-
dians, was a great artist, he was also, like them, a
great interpreter of life. His dramas are satires as
well as poems, and he was and expressed himself
supremely conscious of having a "mission" to fulfil.
"He has scorned from the first," he makes the
chorus sing of himself in the "Peace":

"He has scorned from the first to descend and to dip
Peddling and meddling in private affairs:
To detect and collect every petty defect
Of husband and wife and domestical life;
But intrepid and bold, like Alcides of old,
When the rest stood aloof, put himself to the proof
In his country's behoof." [1]

His aim, in fact, was deliberately to instruct his
countrymen in political and social issues; to attack
the abuses of the Assembly, of the Law-courts and
the home; to punish demagogues, charlatans, professional politicians; to laugh back into their senses
"revolting" sons and wives; to defend the orthodox
faith against philosophers and men of science.
These are the themes that he embodies in his plots,

[1] Aristoph. Peace, 751 *seq.*—Translated by Frere.

and these the morals that he enforces when he
speaks through the chorus in his own person.   And
the result is an art-product more strange to the
modern mind in its union of poetry with prose, of
æsthetic with didactic significance, than even that
marvellous creation, the Greek tragedy.   Of the
character of this comedy the reader may form an
idea through the admirable and easily accessible
translations of Frere,[1] and we are therefore dis-
pensed from the obligation to attempt, as in the
case of tragedy, an account of some particular
specimen of the art.

§ 8. Summary

And here must conclude our survey of the character of Greek art.   The main point which we have
endeavoured to make clear has been so often insisted
upon, that it is hardly necessary to dwell upon it
further.   The key to the art of the Greeks, as well
as to their ethics, is the identification of the beautiful and the good; and it therefore is as natural in
treating of their art to insist on its ethical value as
it was to insist on the æsthetic significance of their
moral ideal.   But, in fact, any insistence on either
side of the judgment is misleading.   The two points
of view had never been dissociated; and art and
conduct alike proceeded from the same imperative
impulse, to create a harmony or order which
was conceived indifferently as beautiful or good.

[1] In Morley's Universal Library.

Through and through, the Greek ideal is Unity. To make the individual at one with the state, the real with the ideal, the inner with the outer, art with morals, finally to bring all phases of life under the empire of a single idea, which, with Goethe, we may call, as we will, the good, the beautiful, or the whole —this was the aim, and, to a great extent, the achievement of their genius. And of all the points of view from which we may envisage their brilliant activity none perhaps is more central and more characteristic than this of art, whose essence is the comprehension of the many in the one, and the perfect reflection of the inner in the outer.

Conclusion

CHAPTER V

CONCLUSION

NOW that we have examined in some detail the most important phases of the Greek view of life, it may be as well to endeavour briefly to recapitulate and bring to a point the various considerations that have been advanced.

But, first, one preliminary remark must be made. Throughout the preceding pages we have made no attempt to distinguish the Greek "view" from the Greek "ideal"; we have interpreted their customs and institutions, political, social, or religious, by the conceptions and ideals of philosophers and poets, and have thus, it may be objected, made the mistake of identifying the blind work of popular instinct with the theories and aspirations of conscious thought.

Such a procedure, no doubt, would be illegitimate if it were supposed to imply that Greek institutions were the result of a deliberate intention consciously adopted and approved by the average man. Like other social products they grew and were not made; and it was only the few who realized fully all that they implied. But on the other hand it is a distinguishing characteristic of the Greek age that the ideal formulated by thought was the direct outcome of the facts. That absolute separation of what ought to be from what is which continues to haunt and vitiate modern life had not yet been made in ancient Greece. Plato, idealist though he be, is yet rooted in the facts of his age; his perfect republic he bases on the institutions of Sparta and Crete; his perfect man he shapes on the lines of the Greek citizen. That dislocation of the spirit which opposed the body to the soul, heaven to earth, the church to the state, the man of the world to the priest, was alien to the normal consciousness of the Greeks. To them the world of fact was also the world of the ideal; the conceptions which inspired their highest aims were already embodied in their institutions and reflected in their life; and the realization of what ought to be involved not the destruction of what was, but merely its perfecting on its own lines.

While, then, on the one hand, it would be ridiculous so to idealize the civilization of the Greeks as to imply that they had eliminated discord and confusion, yet, on the other hand, it is legitimate to say that they had built on the plan of the ideal, and that their life both in public and private was, by the very law of its existence, an effort to realize explicitly that type of Good which was already implicitly embodied in its structure.

The ideal, in a word, in ancient Greece, was organically related to the real; and that is why it is possible to identify the Greek view with the Greek ideal.

Bearing this in mind we may now proceed to

recapitulate our conclusions as to what that view
was. And first, let us take the side of speculation.
Here we are concerned not with the formal systems
of Greek thought, but with that half-unconscious
working of imagination as much as of mind whose
expression was their popular religion. Of this
religion, as we saw, the essential feature was that
belief in anthropomorphic gods, by virtue of which
a reconciliation was effected between man and the
powers whether of nature or of his own soul. Behind phenomena, physical or psychic, beings were
conceived of like nature with man, beings, therefore, whose actions he could interpret and whose
motives he could comprehend. For his imagination,
if not for his intellect, a harmony was thus induced
between himself and the world that was not he. A
harmony! and in this word we have the key to the
dominant idea of the Greek civilization.

For, turning now to the practical side, we find the
same impulse to reconcile divergent elements. That
antithesis of soul and body which was emphasized
in the mediæval view of life and dominates still our
current ethical conceptions, is foreign to the Greek
view of life. Their ideal for the individual included
the perfection of the body; beauty no less than
goodness was the object of their quest, and they believed that the one implied the other. But since the
perfection of the body required the co-operation of
external aids, they made these also essential to their
ideal. Not merely virtue of the soul, not merely
health and beauty of the body, but noble birth,
sufficient wealth and a good name among men, were

included in their conception of the desirable life.
Harmony, in a word, was the end they pursued,
harmony of the soul with the body and of the body
with its environment; and it is this that distinguishes
their ethical ideal from that which in later times has
insisted on the fundamental antagonism of the inner
to the outer life, and made the perfection of the
spirit depend on the mortification of the flesh.

The same ideal of harmony dominates the Greek
view of the relation of the individual to the state.
This relation, it is true, is often described as one in
which the parts were subordinated to the whole; but
more accurately it may be said that they were conceived as finding in the whole their realization. The
perfect individual was the individual in the state;
the faculties essential to his excellence had there
only their opportunity of development; the qualities
defined as virtues had there only their significance;
and it was only in so far as he was a citizen that a
man was properly a man at all. Thus that apposi-
tion between the individual and the state which per-
plexes our own society had hardly begun to define itself in Greece. If on the one hand the state made
larger claims on the liberty of the individual, on the
other, the liberty of the individual consisted in a re-
sponse to the claims. So that in this department
also harmony was maintained by the Greeks between
elements which have developed in modern times
their latent antagonism.

Thus, both in speculation and in practice, in his
relation to nature and in his relation to the state,
both internally, between the divergent elements of

which his own being was composed, and externally between himself and the world that was not he, it was the aim, conscious or unconscious, and, in part at least, the achievement of the Greeks, to create and maintain an essential harmony. The antitheses of which we in our own time are so painfully and increasingly aware, between Man as a moral being and Nature as an indifferent law, between the flesh and the spirit, between the individual and the state, do not appear as factors in that dominant consciousness of the Greeks under whose influence their religion, their institutions and their customary ideals had been formed. And so regarded, in general, un- der what may fairly be called its most essential as- pect, the Greek civilization is rightly described as that of harmony.

But, on the other hand, and this is the point to which we must now turn our attention, this harmony which was the dominant feature in the consciousness of the Greeks and the distinguishing characteristic of their epoch in the history of the world, was never- theless, after all, but a transitory and imperfect at- tempt to reconcile elements whose antagonism was too strong for the solution thus proposed. The fac- tors of disruption were present from the beginning in the Greek ideal; and it was as much by the de- velopment of its own internal contradictions as by the invasion of forces from without that that fabric of magical beauty was destined to fall. These con- tradictions have already been indicated at various points in the text, and it only remains to bring them together in a concluding summary.

On the side of speculation, the religion of the Greeks was open, as we saw, to a double criticism. On the one hand, the ethical conceptions embodied in those legends of the gods which were the product of an earlier and more barbarous age, had become to the contemporaries of Plato revolting or ridiculous. On the other hand, to metaphysical speculation, not only was the existence of the gods unproved, but their mutually conflicting activities, their passions and their caprice, were incompatible with that conception of universal law which the developing reason evolved as the form of truth. The reconciliation of man with nature which had been effected by the medium of anthropomorphic gods was a harmony only to the imagination, not to the mind. Under the action of the intellect the unstable combination was dissolved and the elements that had been thus imperfectly joined fell back into their original opposition. The religion of the Greeks was destroyed by the internal evolution of their own consciousness.

And in the sphere of practice we are met with a similar dissolution. The Greek conception of excellence included, as we saw, not only bodily health and strength, but such a share at least of external goods as would give a man scope for his own self-perfection. And since these conditions were not attainable by all, the sacrifice of the majority to the minority was frankly accepted and the pursuit of the ideal confined to a privileged class.

Such a conception, however, was involved in internal contradictions. For in the first place, even for the privileged few, an excellence which depended on external aids was, at the best, uncertain and problematical. Misfortune and disease were possibilities that could not be ignored; old age and death were imperative certainties; and no care, no art, no organization of society, could obviate the inherent incompatibility of individual perfection with the course of nature. Harmony between the individual and his environment was perhaps more nearly achieved by and for the aristocracy of ancient Greece than by any society of any other age. But such a harmony, even at the best, is fleeting and precarious; and no perfection of life delivers from death.

And, in the second place, to secure even this imperfect realization, it was necessary to restrict the universal application of the ideal. Excellence, in Greece, was made the end for some, not for all. But this limitation was felt, in the development of consciousness, to be self-contradictory; and the next great system of ethics that succeeded to that of Aristotle, postulated an end of action that should be at once independent of the aids of fortune and open alike to all classes of mankind. The ethics of a privileged class were thus expanded into the ethics of humanity; but this expansion was fatal to its essence, which had depended on the very limitations by which it was destroyed.

With the Greek civilization beauty perished from the world. Never again has it been possible for man to believe that harmony is in fact the truth of all existence. The intellect and the moral sense have developed imperative claims which can be satisfied by no experience known to man. And as a consequence of this the goal of desire which the Greeks could place in the present, has been transferred, for us, to a future infinitely remote, which nevertheless is conceived as attainable. Dissatisfaction with the world in which we live and determination to realize one that shall be better, are the prevailing characteristics of the modern spirit. The development is one into whose meaning and end this is not the place to enter. It is enough that we feel it to be inevitable; that the harmony of the Greeks contained in itself the factors of its own destruction; and that in spite of the fascination which constantly fixes our gaze on that fairest and happiest halting-place in the secular march of man, it was not there, any more than here, that he was destined to find an ultimate reconciliation and repose.

INDEX

A.

Achilles, 7, 33, 185
Æschylus, on the punishment of guilt, 25; on Zeus, 53; and Euripides, 229; his Agamemnon, 240
Agamemnon, the, of Æschylus, 240
Alcibiades, and Socrates, 187
Andromache, 173
Apollo, Delphian, 12, 29; in Euripides, 48
Aristophanes, 20, 46; on physical speculations, 56; on communism, 94; on Athenian democracy, 117; on women, 175; on Æschylus and Euripides, 229, 234; character of his comedies, 247
Aristotle, his view of the state, 75; on slaves, 78; on forms of government, 86, 93; on property, 100; his ideal of the state, 131; on artisans, 138; on happiness, 139; on virtue, 147; on pleasure, 157; on women, 175; on painting, 217; on music, 221; on the dance, 223; on the tragic hero, 233
Artisans, 76, 138
Aspasia, 182
Athens, 111
Athletics, 143

B.

Bacchic rites, 30

C.

Citizen, Greek conception of, 71
City-state, 69
Cleomachus, 188
Cleon, 116
Comedy, 246
Communism, in Aristophanes, 94; in Plato, 98
Crœsus, 140

D.

Dancing, 223
Demosthenes, on law, 74, 127; on Athenian demagogues, 124; on sycophants, 125; on marriage, 171, 183
Dionysius, 30; Zagreus, 31, 40
Divination, 18

E.

Education, in Sparta, 105; by poetry, 227
Erinyes, 25
Euripides, his criticism of the myths, 48; on slaves, 81; on Athens, 113; on women, 176-181; and Æschylus, 229

F.

Family, the, 170
Festivals, 13
Friendship, 184

G.

Goethe, on Greek sepulchral monuments, 37

259

Woman, 169; in the Homeric age, 172

machus, 158; on marriage, 170; his ideal of a wife, 179

X.

Xenophon, on the mechanical arts, 138; account of Ischo-

Z.

Zeus, 43, 53; of Pheidias, 144, 214

ANN ARBOR PAPERBACKS *reissues of works of enduring merit*

The University of Michigan Press / Ann Arbor